JUST A COP

**A Memoir of
My 30 Years With The Toronto Police
and As An Undercover Agent**

by
Hal Cunningham

JUST A COP

**A Memoir of
My 30 Years With The Toronto Police
and As An Undercover Agent**

by
Hal Cunningham

Book Cover by *Aeternum Designs*

VP Publication an imprint of
RJ Parker Publishing

ISBN 13: 9781792065880

www.RJParkerPublishing.com

Published in Canada

This book is licensed for your personal enjoyment only. This book may not be re-sold or given away to other people. If you would like to share this book with another person, please purchase an additional copy for each person you share it with. If you're reading this book and did not purchase it, or it was not purchased for your use only, then you should return it to the publisher and purchase your own copy. Thank you for respecting the hard work of this author.

Edited by T.R. Cartwright and Bettye McKee
eBook formatting by www.ebooklaunch.com

While the Publisher is responsible for the sales, marketing and distribution of a book, it is the author's obligation to ensure the accuracy of facts.

I dedicate this book to all the past and present men and women of the Toronto Police Service that also wore the uniform and dedicated their lives to the same calling.

They patrol the same streets 24/7 while you sleep to keep you safe and secure. Their sacrifices and commitment to their community is heroic and, please, the next time you pass one of them, shake their hand and say, "Thank you for your Service."

INTRODUCTION

56 Division

May 25th, 1973, was my tenth day on the job. This young naive 19-year-old had just completed the two-year course of Law and Security at Loyalist College and was hired as an unarmed Uniform Police Cadet with Metro Toronto Police. I was posted to #56 Division on Pape Avenue in downtown Toronto. Talk about a duck out of water! This would also be my tenth day living in Toronto and totally unfamiliar with the entire City. Also, my tenth day away from home for the first time. I was detailed to work the midnight shift, riding escort with the Constables. This was just prior to the implementation of the two-man patrol cars. Most of the Officers appreciated the company and change of pace by having someone with them during the long night shift.

Everyone so far that I worked with were very accommodating and patient with me and trying to assist me in adapting to my new environment.

On this night, I was detailed to work with P.C. Paul Feeney. He was a very energetic copper with a go-get-`em positive attitude. I thought it would be a good night. We were assigned one of those old yellow Ford police cars, without roof lights, a screen or any siren. It did have a "radar light". That's a portable flashlight the shape of a small box which is the battery with a large lens screwed onto the two contacts. The car did have all the markings on the sides as a Metro Police car.

Unknown to us, a three-man team of plainclothesmen were somewhere downtown also. They were in an unmarked car and watching a drug house. A car with three motorcycle gang members pulled up to the house.

These bikers were armed with handguns and planning to go inside and rip the place off. If a shooting was to occur, they didn't care. They wanted that drug money. As they were walking up to the house, they saw the unmarked police car and the Drug Squad coppers, and the vehicle chase was on. These two cars raced down residential side streets, but the bikers could not shake their tail. On several occasions, the rear and right front passengers would lean out the open window, lay their handguns on the door-frame of the car, and fire shots back at the Police Officers. This was a wild shootout on a south-bound street between Queen Street East and Eastern Avenue, all east of Pape Avenue. Meanwhile, only a block away, two innocent guys in a marked #56 Division Scout car were chatting about life in Toronto. There was absolutely no conversation now on our police radio. Its silence was soon to be interrupted.

The two cars involved in this chase made a hard right turn onto Eastern Avenue continuing now west-bound. This was a couple of blocks in front of our westbound marked Police Scout car, also on Eastern Avenue. We saw these two cars sliding sideways onto OUR street, and Paul Feeney said to me, "Here we go. We got a couple of guys racing!"

The cars then turned right again, "O.K., we've got them now. That's a dead-end street!"

It took us a few more seconds to reach that dead-end street and make our right turn towards the end. We rounded the corner and stopped in the middle of this short road. There was a two-story building on our right, and to the left was a hill leading up to the main Toronto railway lines.

Just ahead of us was a parking lot full of fuel trucks and a large garbage bin.

There were two cars near that bin with all the doors left open and unoccupied. BANG! BANG! The plainclothes Police Officers were hiding behind that garbage bin, had their weapons drawn and were yelling "Police"! I heard those first shots as they had travelled from the hillside just over our heads towards that building.

Now this country boy was not a hunter and had never heard a gunshot in his life, but after about 2.5 seconds and two shots, I realized what I had just heard. Paul and I were standing in front of this bright yellow car with the lights from the building and our headlights shining on us. BANG! BANG! BANG! Without a word being spoken by either of us, we ran for the passenger side and got down behind my door. I reached into the car and reached for that portable radar flashlight. We could hear the Plainclothes officers providing us with cover fire and firing many shots towards the hill and the train track area. I now shone the light on that hill, leaning on the roof of our car while Paul leaned on the same roof and fired six of the quickest shots I had ever heard. Ever heard? I had never heard one shot before, let alone dozens. We then crouched on the ground and he reloaded six more shells into his revolver. We still had not spoken a word. This was happening all too quickly. He then said to radio for an Assist. I reached in, grabbed the mic and said TEN 33, 5611, ASSIST A PC, we are being SHOT AT! Then I realized I had no idea where the hell we were. I had to yell, and it took Paul two times for me to understand the words "DIBBLE STREET."

I added this street's name for the dispatcher, and it was now a city-wide ASSIST A PC call. They were starting to come from everywhere.

In those days, you could hear in your own car every word uttered in every division on your radio. You just knew when you could talk in your own division without cutting off your own guy's conversation. The whole City heard this kid's yell for help! The radio was no longer silent.

Paul, with his reloaded .38, headed towards the dumpster after telling me to stay with the car. Not a problem for me. I kept shining the light on that hill while Paul and Plainclothesmen approached and climbed it together. There were none of the shooters in the sight of my flashlight, which was a good thing. They were now on top of the hill and out of view on the tracks. I was hoping my light would help and give them a safe area while climbing. It was now very quiet. In those days, you didn't get the sounds of arriving help from sirens blaring. The first to arrive was a #56 Division officer, Gary Wert. He ran over to my car where I was. I had continued to light up a small portion of the hill.

I will always remember that he took the time to run to me, stop and say, "Are you O.K.?" I told him I was fine and pointed to the direction of the hill, and he ran off into the darkness. Unit after unit then arrived, and all were advised of the situation and they all ran off into the darkness.

Paul returned sometime later and said to his team, "Let's look under these trucks." A police car was positioned with its headlights on the trucks, and sure enough, they got one hiding underneath. A second was captured down the tracks, and the next four hours were spent by the officers checking rooftops in the area.

Gary Wert approached me again later and said, "I have been on the job for ten years so far and this has never happened to me. It will never happen to you again." He was a true gentleman, but he ended up being wrong.

Paul and I returned to the station. Now this was only a few months after Police Constable Leslie Maitland was shot and killed by a bank robber. His unarmed trainee was being chased around the car, while also being shot at by the robber.

It was decided to ignore the fact that I was there and involved in this incident. I continued the rest of the shift with the Staff Sergeant working behind the front desk. The two prisoners were being interviewed on the second floor. Two armoured car guards were sitting in our lobby waiting to be picked up and were nervously looking at each other when the volume upstairs had increased. The prisoners were charged with several counts of attempted murder. The third suspect returned from the United States about a year later.

I went home in the morning and called my parents to tell them about my exciting night. My dear mother said, "That's it. You're coming home!" I said NO! I had worked too hard to get here and live my lifelong dream. Weirdly enough, I was not scared.

I think it happened too quickly, and there was no training at that time to kick in. I had not had any. I have been nervous other times since then, but funnily enough, not that night.

A few months later, I saw Paul with the Sergeant during his Annual Equipment Inspection. When it came to his spare ammo, I remember well he produced about 22 extra bullets out of four different pockets. You are issued six spare bullets.

Welcome to Toronto. You grew up quickly in the big City.

LITTLE BOY LOST

I was five years old in 1959 when my family travelled from Trenton to Toronto to attend my cousin's wedding. The church and reception were in the Queen Street East and Jones area of the inner city. In the evening, we went a few blocks south to a house on Eastern Avenue to continue the celebrations. Later, my parents put me in the back seat of the car to sleep, as did my uncle with a younger cousin in the car ahead of ours. These were different times in the 1950s. I recall walking up on another street not knowing where I was or how I got there. Two ladies took me into their house and fed me milk and cookies and called the Police. I had no idea where I had walked away from. A single officer from #56 Division arrived. This would have been only two years after the 1957 amalgamation with the five boroughs to form the new Metropolitan Toronto Police Force. Since I couldn't assist the officer, he loaded me into the front seat of his bright yellow police car and was about to drive me to his Pape Avenue Police station.

On route, I asked him to stop and drive down one street I thought had looked familiar. He did so, and then I recognized our car parked with many others on the street. A knock at the door produced a very surprised and embarrassed father.

Now 14 years later, as a young 19-year-old man, I was starting my first real job as an unarmed Police Cadet and was posted to #56 Division with the Metropolitan Toronto Police Force. Ten days later, at approximately 2 a.m., I was being shot at only two blocks from that wedding party house on Eastern Avenue.

My 30 years with Toronto Police involved downtown uniform Constable duties, Undercover Intelligence/Surveillance assignments, and for the second half, Supervisor duties as a Sergeant and then Staff Sergeant. I did my job to the best of my abilities and am proud of the fine men and women I was fortunate to be able to work with. We had each other's back, and they most likely would have even more stories of interest than mine other than the fact that I have chosen to write them down.

I never knew why I said all during primary, secondary school and college that I wanted to be a policeman. I just always said that that was my goal.

It wasn't until a few years ago that I linked that little lost boy and his eyes being opened to be the start of my interest in his future. I reached that goal and was fortunate enough to find my calling in entering the surveillance field.

This was my chosen career.

CONTENTS

Introduction

Chapter One: As a Cadet and Constable

Chapter Two: As an Undercover Intelligence Agent

Chapter Three: Returning to Uniform/CIB Duties After Intelligence

Chapter Four: As a Sergeant and Staff Sergeant

Conclusion

CHAPTER ONE

AS A CADET and CONSTABLE (1973-1979)
No. 56 Division, Police Cadet (1973)
No. 55 Division, Police Cadet (July 1973)
No. 52 Division, Constable (1975)

THE FIRST DAY: May 15th, 1973.

1973. You are with the Metropolitan Toronto Police Force, but anywhere you go in North America, you just say "Metro" and "they know"! You just got a 18 percent pay increase and are making around $8,000. Home is now #56 Division on Pape Avenue, and like most stations, there is no parking for your personal vehicle. Your car is parked on the residential side streets or sidewalk, and you leave your Toronto Police Street Guide in the window. This is so that some passing Green Hornet PEO (Parking Enforcement Officer) riding a Pie Wagon (3-wheel motorcycle) with a death wish does not tag your personal car while you are working. It is the summer, and your Platoon has two Staff Sergeants and three separate sections to allow for different days off. Everyone is present on the odd Friday as there is a huge overlap. All the cars and all the foot beats are filled on those days.

The summer uniform is a long-sleeved grey shirt with the top button done up and a clip-on tie, Sam Brown belt and strap for the prisoners to throw you around, cross-draw flap holster, and a handcuff pouch. All your leather must be spit polished, especially your boots. Those not regimentally inclined buy Leather Lustre (a black glossy paint) and dry their gear in their dust-free oven.

For the overly promotionally inclined, they buy expensive patent leather. The Parading Sergeant must see his waxed handlebar moustache in your boots, and you must use black dye on a Q-tip to darken the newly punched holes on your belt and cross strap. You have a 12-inch wooden baton inside the special right leg pocket of your pants and usually your own black leather sap in your left rear pocket because we were fighters, and this was a more discreet weapon for offence. Did I forget to mention your hat is screwed on your head 24/7 in and out of the car? Of course, there was no body armour back then. You were given your freshly printed copy of the Hot Sheet with the most recent stolen vehicle list.

We had about 20 yellow marked POLICE assigned cars in the combined #56-55 Divisions. Only two of these cars had a single red light and prisoner screen, and they were not equipped with sirens. The rest had no sirens, no roof light(s), no prisoner screens, a one channel city-wide band radio. It had a single toggle switch to switch over to a Records band for checks on persons or cars. The Records Clerk had a manual rotating file card system at HQ.

On emergency calls, you, usually alone on a one-man car, had to flash the headlights, honk the horn continually, steer the car down the wrong side of the street and operate the radio. Again, there was no top light(s) or siren. Traffic Accident cars did have two red flashing lights and a small dented wail siren, the dents caused by using their wooden issued batons to unfreeze it in the winter months.

Divisional officers were not allowed to investigate PIs (Personal Injury Motor Vehicle Accident), so every PD (Property Damage Motor Vehicle Accident) call was somehow turned into a PI, requiring an Accident car. Those were the days of whiplash. The Traffic/Accident cars did use their sirens to arrive 30 minutes after the fact to take the necessary report. Most of the cars did not have prisoner screens. This meant that the driver was usually getting a boot in the back of the head, either by the prisoner or the shiny Leather Lustre boot of his partner. This occurred while he was vaulting over the back of the front seat to "restrain" the prisoner. Later the screens saved more prisoners from injuries from the police than policemen from being injured by the prisoners.

Minimum requirements stated you must be at least 5'7" and 160 pounds to be hired. The cars have bench seats, and you might be the passenger with your knees in your chest and a slouched posture to allow for the hat on in the car if your 5'7" partner was driving. PWs (Police Women) are not allowed on general patrol. They either work in the Women's Bureau, transporting female prisoners, or the Youth Bureau. They make the same wages as the men and carry their gun and handcuffs in their shoulder-strap purse. Their uniform consists of a white blouse and a skirt with granny boots.

We worked 8-hour shifts and the 3-11 and 4-12 afternoon shifts meant a rush to our favourite police bar 'til the 1 a.m. closing. LIFE WAS GOOD. Times have changed.

CADET

The under-21 years of age Police Cadet Training Program was an integral part of the MTPD and TPS. At 21 years of age, many of us graduated from this initiation into the world of Big City Policing and into the profession of being a full Police Constable. Many of the young men and women that served as Police Cadets were almost guaranteed to move forward and be fully sworn in when they became 21 years old. You had to commit a very serious infraction to get the boot prior to being moved up in your career. I was a young 19 years old and in front of Police Doctor Homonylo. He had his own office at 590 Jarvis Street, Police HQ, and had a lot of inherited power. After he commented on my 153-pound weight, he told me I had a year and a half to get up to the required 160 pounds, or I'd be let go. I was then hired, and my starting salary was just over $8,000 in 1973.

You had no choice and were assigned to one of three postings: Divisional Cadet, Traffic Cadet or Summons Bureau Cadet. It was like passing the NYPD Police Academy and then being told you were either in the NYPD proper, Transit Police or Port Authority Police units. You did not have a say in the choice.

I lucked out and was in a division where I walked the beat, wrote parking tickets with the PEOs around Greenwood Race Track, did the odd school crossing, and rode escort on the scout cars with a platoon officer.

Often the Officers would pass me their leather saps to carry when we worked together, so I ended up buying my own and carried it when I was on patrol duties with the Officers. I didn't like them giving me their equipment which I felt they needed more than I did. I just made sure the Sergeant never saw it, so I could make it to be here on my 21st birthday. We had some good fights and arrests, and I learned a lot with those men (no women there at that time). There were divisional Harley Davidsons, but I was never trained. I did have my Blue Card (Police Driver's License) and drove for the odd PC (Police Constable) on patrol. Traffic Cadets mostly performed motorcycle duties, and Summons Cadets were driving those Beetles and Pintos and delivered the mail/summonses.

Regardless of the postings, ALL learned responsibilities, discipline, accountability, and pride in performing their tasks. This training gave us years of experience on the job ahead of the upcoming PC training. I would admit that there was an attitude at Aylmer (Ontario Police College) from the former Cadets turned PC over the newly hired PCs. Why not! They had all this time spent and exposure to the system over the others.

I was still 153 pounds at the age of 21 and was not fired. They knew they had an investment in me, and I can give return on their product. I made the 160 pounds a few years later. I wish I was still there! Thank goodness I bought back this year and a half of pensionable time, so I started when I was 19 and retired 30 years and 3 months later when I was 49 years old.

After my retirement, I bought a large boat and named it FREEDOM 49. Most people got it.

Look at how many excellent Police Officers we know of that graduated from the Cadet Program.

A YONGE SHOOTER

Now as a young Police Constable, I had just reported off duty from the day shift (7 a.m.-3 p.m.) in #52 Division. It was in September of 1976 when I changed into my civilian clothes for the subway ride home. I threw on my jeans and a short sleeve summer shirt, and then inserted my issued .38 Colt revolver into the pancake holster on my belt under the shirt. I had those oversized wooden aftermarket grips we bought so it would fit a larger hand. No, I didn't go for those custom squeeze-the-mold wooden grips to get those special fitted ones with the finger notches.

It was a short ride to the Wellesley subway at Yonge Street. I walked north on Yonge Street, passing the corner sports stores of Hercules, ABC and Nick's Sporting Goods. I passed the Gasworks Tavern at the corner of Yonge and Dundonald. BANG! When I was one short block north at Gloucester Street, I reached my corner. I probably was thinking, "Maybe this is the year for the Maple

Leafs to win again." BANG! I turned to walk east towards my apartment building where I lived with Wife #1.

I was just crossing the parkette over the Yonge subway and saw a Police car racing towards me. BANG! An afternoon shift officer from #52 Division stopped, and I warned him of my approach to his car. He then recognized me and advised that there was sniper just above us on the roof of #15 Dundonald Street. We looked up to the top of this approximately 25-floor apartment building and there he was! He was leaning over the edge pointing his long rifle with a scope down towards the street.

My gun was now out as I didn't want this guy taking the 60 seconds to come down, use one of many exit doors and surprise me. I don't like surprises! The Officer ran towards the building, and I had asked him to leave his car unlocked and open so I could listen to his radio. I watched a second officer pull his yellow marked vehicle into the small circular driveway at the front of #15 Dundonald Street. The sniper then leaned again over the side of the roof and pointed his gun at the vehicle. He set his sights on the car when the Officer was exiting the vehicle for the front doors. I held my breath and for some unknown reason he did not shoot. I was glad as he was now safely inside.

A little dark Horizon (unmarked Police car) pulled up behind the police vehicle I was using as cover. Two plainclothesmen from #51 Division heard the call and had responded. I think they were uniform officers working a Warrant type car on the day shift. Their spring jackets were hiding their holsters.

Each approached me, drew their guns and asked for a situation report. We could see this sniper take the occasional shot down towards Yonge Street.

The driver of this car then put his arms on the roof of our police car and started to sight in on the sniper with his .38 revolver. We could clearly see apartment residents on their balconies just below the shooter trying to look up towards the roof. As this was a very long, impossible and very dangerous shot, I looked at this fellow and said, "Don't even think of it!" He then complied, and they also ran the dangerous open gauntlet towards the apartment building.

I remained behind the police car at the parkette yelling at people trying to cross this kill zone, "Police Officer, get off the street!" I yelled at the people on their balconies from the Gloucester apartment building, "Police Officer, get off your balconies!" They were looking directly across at the shooter. Since I could see the shooter, he could see me. I thought it might not have been the best move to yell in my Aylmer (Police College) voice, giving myself away in this echo chamber between these two large buildings, but I felt the warnings were more important. I had decided the inside was being addressed by my four brave on-duty Brothers. I had felt it was my place to ensure no one was exposed in the gauntlet or balconies.

I had been listening to the police radio. These were the days of the flaming cards on the dispatcher's conveyor, Sergeant of Communications and the odd penalty box P.C. on a dispatch desk.

These were the days of that loud, arrogant, authoritative, accented dispatcher Jim Shaw. He was a take-charge dispatcher that told all officers what to do and not to do daily. It was a confrontational day when he was on your divisional radio-desk, but it was a GREAT day when the feces hit the fan and he was the dispatcher you then wanted. Mr. Shaw was not on our desk that shift, and the Sergeant of Communications then got on the air and took command.

I knew that strong Englishman's accented voice and recalled I met him a few years earlier when he was a P.C. at #55 Division. I forget his name, but he was a tall, thin man and had a great sense of humour at any after-work get-together. He was a party guy then, but all business now. He said, "ETF3 (Emergency Task Force Gun Truck), go directly to Yonge and Wellesley, and ETF3A, go to the heliport at Cherry and Unwin. Get up over that guy and stop him!" My mind immediately visualized the crashing of a helicopter down on Wellesley and Yonge. I then heard, because of the shots fired, there were multiple injured parties on Yonge Street now.

Now that there were at least four Officers in the building, they implemented the 1976 MTP Active Shooter Policy. Well, since that policy hadn't been developed (to come about 35 years later), they knew that common sense said they had to get up there now and apprehend, meaning stop and most likely kill this guy. Time could not allow waiting for the ETF. I heard on the radio it was now over.

The four had reached the roof and the sniper's final shot was into his own head. Shortly after, I walked the rest of the way home and caught the six o'clock news.

It seems this Cuckoo for Cocoa Puffs chap had just had his butt stamped as "sane" and ready to return to society by the Clarke Mental Institute on Spadina Avenue. He went directly to one of those sporting goods stores on the corner and immediately bought his new high-power rifle, scope and ammunition. It was a short walk out that door and around the corner to #15 Dundonald Street, and shooting off the lock to the roof was too easy.

His shots on the streets below injured seven people. Apparently, not one citizen was struck by a bullet directly. They were all injured by flying pieces of asphalt scooped up by the bullets giving them injuries to their lower extremities. Surprise, surprise, in 1978 the previously stalled Firearm Acquisition Certificates (FACs) Bill was finally passed in Government.

I looked at those scoop marks in the road and sidewalk for many years to follow. Bottom line…ALL Officers went home at the end of their shifts to their first wives.

NOTE: Early September 1976. Yonge Street north of Wellesley. Ernest Lamourandire was the shooter. He bought the .303 rifle one-half hour before he started shooting. He was released from the Clarke Mental Institute a day or two before the shooting.

THE SHOWER

One day a lady shot at us in downtown Toronto. It was a day shift as we were working in the old #52 Division (149 College Street station) when a call came in about a woman threatening to kill herself. Three one-man yellow cars responded. Myself and Constables Paul Carey and George Gadsdon (aka Dog Face) attended the scene. We parked out front of the Elmwood Women's Residence on Elm Street in the Dundas and Yonge area. We entered and were met by the lady manager. She advised us of a female tenant on the third floor that had expressed a desire to kill herself. The four of us went to the third floor where she pointed out the exact door to the one-room hotel unit.

I think there might have been about a total of 6 or 7 years combined years of experience between the three of us, as we were all rookies. We did know enough not to stand in front of the door. George used the manager's pass key and gently put it into the slot. Just as he was about to turn the key, BANG, one very loud shot. Now Hal was starting to get used to these shots in downtown Toronto and knew this was not some little handgun. It was very loud and perhaps was a long gun of some sort. The bullet came through a wall somewhere in the apartment, close enough to make us draw our handguns from our cross-draw flap holsters and duck!

Paul dove for the fire door with the long metal push bar. Dog Face and I grabbed the manager and ran her down the hall and ejected her into the stairs we had just used to come up. Paul's door was locked, and he had to run down the hall south towards us. Dog Face then jumped into an open doorway across the hallway.

I was in a doorway with a bead on the shooter's door and ready to act if anything popped out. Dog Face had jumped into a room that ended up being the ladies' shower room for that floor and Yes! there was a lady in the shower! Paul positioned himself behind me, and I instructed him to call the ETF (Emergency Task Force). In those days, scout car officers were not issued portable radios. They were only for our beat officers. Paul was heading back down to his car to call for help. We were aware that the ETF was nearby. There was some Olympic event at Varsity Stadium which they had been assigned to work.

Dog Face came out of the shower room and joined me in a doorway at the south end of the hallway. Now we both had a bead on that door. We were ready if anybody opened it. He had to tell me about his shower room adventure, and because of the nervous and stressful situation, we both got the "giggles."

I recall taking my handgun out of my right hand and placing it temporarily into my left hand while I wiped the sweat off my palm. The wooden grips made for a poor grip when your hand got wet. Two weeks after this incident, I had new rubber grips that made the grip better if you had a sweaty hand.

We must have waited there about 10 to 20 long minutes until the ETF arrived. Their five-man team slid along the wall towards the door. This was prior to headsets years later, and one of their portable radios blasted out a conversation, giving away their stealth approach. The key was still in the closed door, and they then opened it and there she was.

She had fired off her high-power rifle but only after she had shot the same bullet through her own neck first. I take a bullet coming at me personally and don't question its path. To my surprise, she was still alive and was taken away to the hospital. She did become a quadriplegic and had some very serious injuries. I don't know for how long she survived those injuries, but her life had changed.

I only know we protected the manager and Dog Face's new friend in the shower.

INITIATION

The Rookie had to survive the initiation. We were working out of old #52 Division at 149 College Street, and if you were new, you walked a beat, especially on the midnight shift. I recall walking alone in the back laneways of Queen Street and Yorkville all summer checking doors and fire escapes.

It was a challenge to find an insecure on your beat and report it. After about a year, you were solo on a scout car as a new class of recruits was coming out of the College every six months. You transformed quickly from Roger Rookie to Victor Veteran, at least in your own mind. Now it was pay back time for the new guys to feel the pain.

The new guy on our shift was Greg. He was a nice young man but a little different than the usual mold and his own man. If you were assigned a beat on midnights, "Sergeant's Rules" dictated you were required to walk to and from your post, including for your lunch back at the station. I was driving along Yorkville and saw Greg up ahead walking his post when he saw the big yellow police car approaching him. He looked up and waved at me. The wave clearly said to me, "Hey, it's 2 a.m., please drive me in for my lunch." I was in a funny mood and was now driving on the sidewalk. He then noticed it was me behind the wheel, and he started to run away, fearing the big chrome bumper. He may have "gently" bounced off my hood as I returned to the street portion of the roadway and drove off.

I continued to patrol my area thinking the rookie just learned a lesson; maybe that I'm unpredictable?

About a half hour later, I was driving past our police station and saw a big yellow Zamboni-size City of Toronto Street Cleaning machine making a U turn in front of #149 College Street. As it stopped at the curb, out of the upper fly bridge cabin crawled out P.C. Greg. He had commandeered the driver to take him to the station for his lunch. I thought, Roger Rookie has just graduated. He will be O.K.

A year later, we were now at the new #52 Division on Dundas Street. Greg and I were assigned to work together one night on a south end #52 Division scout car. We had attended a domestic call where we arrested the boyfriend for hitting his girlfriend several times. At first, she looked a lot worse than she was, so I escorted her in the ambulance to the hospital, while Greg transported Buddy to the station under arrest.

An hour later, I attended the station to advise the Investigators she only had minor injuries. I was walking towards the 2nd floor Detective office just as Greg was escorting the accused from the washroom back towards the office. Greg started the conversation by saying, "Hal, how is she?" I don't know why this happens but, without losing a beat and while I showed a very stern look, I immediately replied, "Greg. She died!"

I will always remember the look on Buddy's face as his eyes rolled up towards our new ceiling and as his knees buckled and he melted to the floor.

Officer Greg was standing in shock with the prisoner's arm still being held up in the air in the "prisoner escort" holding position and Buddy laid out on our new clean concrete floor.

I panicked and decided to go downstairs. A few minutes later, I could hear one of our fine Detectives yelling throughout the station, "Cunningham! Cunningham!"

I'm not sure if he married her or not, but I do think his abusive days may have ended that night. You're welcome!

ID CARDS

At one time the only Police Identification we had was a small plastic card inside our personal wallets. Unless you were a Plainclothesman, you only had this simple card in your wallet like a health card or library card. I also vaguely recall a round yellow piece of plastic that had TTC on it. This was your plainclothes-issued TTC pass for on-duty work only.

Many of us young uniform guys bought our own badge and wallet from the Ontario Police Association. I did as our own Police Service would not issue us the proper ID for when you were off duty.

When I was transferred to Plainclothes assignments, I was issued the proper badge and wallet with "Plainclothes or Plainclothesman" on the bottom where normally a badge number would have been placed.

I believe it was in the early 1980s when they finally lined us up at our stations and issued us our own wallets and badges. This was our history to get where we are today.

CHEQUE-MATE

In those days, Staff Sergeants and Sergeants were like gods. One of my first Sergeants was Sgt. Mike DREW at #55 Division. Most Sergeants also tend to have a sign-off at the end of the parade. Sgt. Drew would close the parade with "Be safe out there, and if I don't get anyone coming in to complain about you, then I know you are not doing your job." I think he meant it. There was also a strict procedure when booking off duty. After depositing your tickets and summonses in their boxes, you stood in front of the Staff Sergeant, at attention, held up your memo book and always stated, "Reporting off duty Staff, no further reports!" You clicked your two heels together. He would look up and announce, "Dismissed." Now your day was done, with his blessing.

Staff Sgt. Colin Campbell was one of my two "Staffs" on my platoon at #52 Division. He was affectionately known as C.C. or 164B, which was the L.C.B.O. stock number for Canadian Club. It seemed like once every six months for five years, he would catch me in the hallway and say, "Psst... Come here! How is your wife and kids?" I would reply "Fine, sir, but I don't have any kids."

This was his way of trying to connect, at arm's length, with his men. Maybe the shifts were too big back then, but he was trying. The other Staff Sergeant was John Bremner. A true gentleman in all ways.

I recall one afternoon shift when we arrived, there was a rumour that our platoon might lose him because our traffic enforcement workload was too low, in a comparison with the other platoons.

I canvassed our platoon before parade, and every one of us went out that night and hit everything moving downtown while leaving the minor pending calls for others. We would walk on broken glass for that man. That was the last we ever heard of that rumour. I also fondly recall him practicing his bagpipes on Sunday mornings in the empty cells, echoing throughout the station.

There was a Staff Sergeant at #51 Division that adopted another management style. He was very autocratic, and his criticisms were not always valid. It did not go over well, and the officers reacted. The Staff Sergeant kept calling Payroll for months, wondering why he hadn't received his paycheques. It was now believed that perhaps, after the courier dropped off the entire paycheques for the station, that his cheque was being fed to "Ernie" the Shredder.

From that point on, he had arranged for his cheques to be sent to neighbouring #55 Division and picked up personally. He later made the mistake of confiding with a member of his inside staff that he was concerned that, since there was a history of Alzheimer's in his family, he also might develop it.

His shift waited a few weeks, and on the next day shift, they removed his car keys, drove his personal vehicle back home and put the keys back. When this Staff Sergeant finished his shift, they watched him wandering in the parking lot looking for his car. He eventually returned inside, and they told him, "Staff, don't you remember, you rode the TTC today to test out your travel time?" You don't mess with the boys from #51 Division.

I always avoided the front desk and Supervisors and hit the road as soon as possible to get to my office, "the road." That way, they didn't get to know me too well. I was rewarded one day.

I returned to #52 Division mid-shift using the back door. I could hear and see my Platoon Sergeant at the front desk dealing with an irate citizen. It was then that I saw the Sergeant physically eject the man out the front door, and he said, "I know that officer and Cunningham wouldn't do that!" I had a "pucker" moment and quietly and swiftly retreated out the back door and back to my office, the car. I had thought that old Sergeant Drew, from many years earlier, would have been proud of me.

I always respected the rank, and years later, as a Supervisor myself, adjusted to the new "Y" generation. Say no more, times did change in many ways and so did we.

1975- Graduated the Ontario Police College, Basic Constable Training. (21 years old)

A MUTUAL HOMICIDE

I recall my first Homicide arrest. It was a summer's evening and the usual, a call to a rooming house over an argument. This old house was one of several on Mutual Street south of Carlton in #52 Division. My partner and I were trying to deal with a group of intoxicated tenants in a first-floor apartment. I always remember his name: Bond (like in James Bond). He and his girlfriend were loaded and not getting along. She lived in the house next door but continued to drink with him, and the usual argument followed. She complained to me about his conduct, and I advised her to stay in her own house and avoid him. She then said, "He is going to kill me!" I remember giving her the benefit of my vast couple years of wisdom and experience and said to her, "He's not going to kill you!" I figured her problems were self-inflicted, and if she feared her boyfriend, then maybe she would stop getting drunk with him. I don't think anything I could have said would have changed their situation. We left and returned to the wild streets of downtown to cruise Yonge Street.

Maybe a couple of months and a hundred radio calls later, I had just started an afternoon shift when the Hotshot came in. It was for a Double Homicide at a rooming house on Mutual Street. As we arrived, the address looked familiar. This was the rooming house of Mr. Bond.

We were met by the building manager. He said he hadn't heard from Mr. Bond all day and looked in the side window as the door was still locked. He saw the two bodies in the bed and called the Police.

We used his key and slowly and carefully looked inside. There was a dead-looking Mr. Bond and his girlfriend on the bed. A quick view of the room showed a television still running, alcohol on the table and, other than it being a dump, nothing else out of place. I moved a few steps closer to the bed and now saw her throat had been slashed and a large quantity of blood had dried around her head. I touched her exposed foot and it was white, very cold and stiff. Yup, she was dead!

I couldn't see his injuries yet.

My mind started racing. Holy shit! He did kill her! Is this a problem for Hal? Seal the scene and make the notifications. Now my quick thought process was suddenly interrupted to my surprise. Mr. Bond let out a loud snore. He was alive! It now changed to one murder and a drunk. He had obviously murdered her and fell asleep for the night beside his Honey. It was best we get him out of the crime scene and in custody. We lifted this limp body and carried him by the hands and feet down the hallway to the front door. Now I could hear the approaching sirens of the ambulance and the firemen. I was about to have 6 to 8 emergency workers stomp into my first murder scene. I knew I was in charge and responsible and wanted to protect MY scene.

While on the front lawn, we were almost to the scout car with a limp Mr. Bond when I let his feet go. He dropped to the ground leaving my partner holding his two arms in the air and Mr. Bond's body on the little green lawn. I ran to the front door and blocked the entrance to stop these guys from entering.

I told them we had an obviously deceased woman in the bedroom, and I wanted one, and only one, ambulance guy to enter carefully with me to confirm death. I ensured he took only about four planned steps into the room, so he could also touch her foot. He looked at her neck and then felt her foot. Yup, she was long dead, and we stepped four steps back to the door. The next police officer arrived, and I requested he guard the main house door and don't let anyone in, especially the guys with the big boots and axes.

Mr. Bond was taken to the station and placed in an interview room. He was charged with her murder. I had sketched the entire apartment in my book, as taught at the College. I tried to make sure I didn't mess this up. Of course, I passed on my knowledge of the earlier call to this address.

To my surprise, that was the last I ever heard of the case against Mr. Bond, no court card, nothing! My first Homicide pinch. It wasn't pretty, but we don t get a choice, do we? I did immediately solve the case, though.

THE ENEMY WITHIN

Once I made an enemy of the Detective Sergeant in charge of the biggest Criminal Investigative Bureau with Metro Police, and he threatened to get me.

My partner and I were on midnight patrol duties in downtown #52 Division. It was around 2 a.m. when we were dispatched to back up another car at a business alarm near Dundas Street East and Church Street. Paul and Andy were already on scene, and we just had to confirm that the premise was secure.

Stu and I were back in our car writing in our memo books and saw Paul and Andy drive off in the laneway. They stopped their police car approximately one block south of us, but still in the alley. One short minute later, we could hear yelling from the location of their car. We cruised forward towards their location and saw a man standing there yelling at them. We found out that the two officers had decided to relieve themselves in the privacy of the rear laneway. They had been urinating on a large pile of cardboard boxes when suddenly a man sat up and yelled at them. He had been sleeping under the pile of boxes. This was a hot summer's night and not at all what anyone expected. He took great exception to be urinated on and wasn't shy about voicing his displeasure. Paul and Andy tried to explain to the man that this was totally unintentional and apologized for this happening. Stu and I tried to calm the man down, but he would not stop yelling, and we gave up. He was dressed like a street person and was very dirty in his appearance.

The man told us that he was the owner of the office building that we all were standing behind. Nothing the four of us could say would calm him down, so we all decided to move on.

A few hours later, things downtown started to get quiet, and we decided to see the Sergeant and request the rest of the shift off to go home and sleep.

Unknown to us, Paul and Andy had also taken time off to go home early.

It was during a very deep sleep around 10 a.m. when the phone beside my bed rang and woke me up. A buddy from my shift said, "Were you in a laneway off Dundas Street last night and met an old man sleeping in a pile of garbage?"

I knew enough by then to not answer and asked, "Why?" I was then advised the entire midnight shift was kept on duty after their shift on overtime and forced to stand in a Police lineup. Apparently, our old man alleged he had been beaten up by police officers in a back alley overnight. The Detective Sergeant in charge of the Investigative office, also know as the D.S., was conducting a Criminal Investigation into the matter. My buddy told me this was highly unusual to be forced into a lineup, and the D.S. walked the man down the Police line and was ticked off when he couldn't identify anyone. He apparently yelled at the man several times, "They must be here. Pick them out!" The officers were not very pleased with being subjected to this procedure and his behaviour. I didn't go back to sleep that morning.

I returned to work that evening with Stu, Paul, Andy, and the rest of our shift. No one approached us or asked us any questions, and that was the last we heard of the matter for some time. I did hear that the Investigation revealed that this man went to a party and was involved in a fight.

That is where he was assaulted but tried to blame the police later. He, in fact, did own the building that he decided to pass out behind in the pile of boxes.

Due to the fact they had evidence that he was beat up elsewhere and had lied about it, the D.S. and his Investigators had charged him with Public Mischief for making a false allegation.

It was maybe a month or two later that the D.S. called me into his office. He had found out that there were four policemen at the back of the business talking to the man that night. I was asked by him, "Why didn't you tell us you guys were there that night?" I took a major stand as a young copper standing up to a Detective Sergeant and said, "Sir, I heard how you were acting that morning and out for blood, pushing the complainant to identify and charge a copper, so I wasn't about to jump up and say, PICK ME!" He didn't like that answer and I didn't care. He was told it was a total coincidence that the four of us independently decided to take time off and go home to bed. Inside, I thought, "Some investigator, maybe they should have checked to see if any members of the platoon had booked off early!" The D.S. now said, "Cunningham, I'm going to get you if it's the last thing I do!"

I thought my career was screwed and I will have this over me forever. That was the last I ever heard of it.

A few years later, the D.S. would be called by some a hero for giving himself up as a hostage during a bank robbery at King and Yonge Street. Some police sources said his actions were against all procedures and hampered the negotiations.

I commenced an undercover career a few years later and heard he had passed away. I don't like being threatened and bullied and knew that I had outlived the threat and the potential cloud hanging over my head.

CHAPTER TWO

AS AN UNDERCOVER INTELLIGENCE AGENT (1979 - 1984)

Intelligence Bureau, Mobile Support Services (M.S.S.) Detective Constable

Royal Canadian Mounted Police (R.C.M.P.), National Criminal Intelligence Section (N.C.I.S.), attached to the Witness Protection Program

At just 25 years old, I was one of the youngest officers to be accepted at Mobile Support Services (M.S.S.) This is the undercover surveillance unit for Intelligence Services. All surveillance requests to follow major suspects in high profile crimes is to be only done by M.S.S. This includes, but is not limited to, following murder suspects, bank robbers, murderers, terrorists, drug dealers and many other types of criminals. The first thing that occurred there was my identity was changed from Constable #4741 to Agent #34. From that moment on, all correspondence and radio communications referred to me as Agent #34. Your contacts with your former officers are lost as you are told to not discuss your assignments with them, and they have been told to not acknowledge you when they see you in public. The location of your undercover office is not to be revealed.

You are required to turn in your regular .38 revolver for a short 2-inch barrel .38 that fits down the back of your pants. Most times it was in my briefcase in the back seat of the car. Leaving it in the car allowed you to go without a jacket or being able to take it off at any time during surveillance. I was assigned to a team to learn, over the next six months, the skills involved in all aspects of mobile and foot surveillance techniques. I worked with Agents #42, #22 and #20. They were the best and made me what I am today. Months later, when I became proficient, I could provide "payback." The four of us could follow anyone, anywhere, anytime without ever being noticed.

The fast-paced driving was an absolute rush, and we all could turn a good wheel. Each day was like street racing, but under the radar. Agent #20 (aka Daneen Rae) was my favourite. She was the most confident operative on foot and driving I had ever seen. She would be my female escort, or more appropriately, I would be her male escort when we went on foot together in restaurants or elsewhere. I remember her from 1974 when she was one of the first policewomen to be reassigned to armed uniform street duties in #55 Division. It was a sad time when the world lost her (and her/our good friend Constable Louise Lehman, Agent #15) to leukemia and cancer a few years later.

THE HYDRO CASTLE

Long before there was a 21 Jump Street, we had this abandoned hydro facility on Chaplin Crescent that resembled a small castle tower over a parking garage. This was the secret home of MSS for a couple of dozen young Undercover Operators. I was only 25 years old, had reached First Class PC, passed my promotional exam and was the youngest officer to be taken into this specialized unit. These were the days when a cigar-chomping Bert Novice would push his Hold Up Squad requests for a surveillance team. That meant working his project and taking with me the 18-inch pistol grip shotgun along the side of my Camaro's bucket seat for the day. It could result in a later possible shoot-out with the Dirty Tricks gang on Laird Drive. It could also be another shoot-out on Blackcreek Drive after watching a bank robbery go down. The Hold Up Squad would blow by our undercover cars with an Ingram machine gun sticking out the passenger window and firing in a 1930s Chicago style. A very young and sharp Drug Squad team of Kim Derry and Billy Blair (later to be Chief) would result in me getting my white parka for a full day of laying in a York Region snowbank with binoculars watching a farmhouse/biker lab. Then there were the projects watching and filming Mob Father Michael Racco and his psycho son Domenic outside their St. Clair Bakery having an outdoor "Soprano" New Jersey-style secret pow-wow.

It could mean driving halfway to Montreal to meet Mob Boss Frank Controni's car and follow him all over Toronto and sitting at the next table to listen to his conversation with boxer-turned-enforcer Eddie Melo.

Life was watching a homicide on the news and the next morning being requested by the Homicide Squad to follow their Number One suspect. One day you are watching and listening to a meet between a Biker/Mob Enforcer and Mob Boss Cosimo Commisso where they are planning a double hit. The next day, you are required to live with the biker with an Uzi machine gun (in a gym bag or briefcase) beside my right knee for the next year on the Witness Protection Program. All other days were the most intense Street Grand Prix driving broken up by stints of foot work. You were required to act like the average Joe, ensuring you did not draw any attention to yourself or your team. This was the daily routine of these UNSUNG HEROES I was so lucky to work with. I only hope that our current members are also able to achieve that career within policing you were always meant to do. Our fellow retired members also enjoyed the extreme satisfaction achieved by doing your own personal tasks the best you could.

Thank you, MSS, for helping me reach my personal Everest.

Undercover Intelligence Agent #34 (1979-1984)

THE JOKER

    Every Unit had that one practical joker. Ours in my time in Intelligence was Bob K. Don't ever turn your back on him.

    Our team was watching an address in #54 Division when I cruised into the McDonald's Drive-Thru to pick up a quick lunch. Unknown to me, Mr. K. was sitting in the same lot to cover that area near our address. I cranked my crystal down and approached the speaker. I was about to ask for my Big Mac when a LOUD voice boomed through my surveillance radio that was installed under my seat. It wasn't my crew advising our target was out and moving. It was the clown yelling my order, "I'll have 48 Big Macs, 27 orders of large fries and 12 milkshakes!" Shit! I dove my right hand under the seat to shut the radio off and then explained to the speaker lady that I needed to amend my order. I looked around, and there he was hidden in the lot laughing in his car.

He could be serious at times. Up in Sault Ste. Marie, we had followed a drug dealer and watched him as he took his delivery from across the U.S. side of the river. Mr. K. was parked alone in an open field as the "target" drove by slowly to check him out. He embraced and made passionate love to his rolled-up winter coat with the nice fur collar. The embarrassed dealer looked away and carried on.

One day on the way to work, Craig K. had his coat and badge slip off his seat strap and they were demolished in the motorcycle chain. He submitted a 149 (memo) to the Inspector for a new replacement badge.

Bob K. was working the midnight shift as our Office Security/Office Janitor and saw the memo on the Staff Sergeant's desk. He gently inserted it into the Olivetti and typed one additional line and returned it to the boss's desk mail tray. The next day, poor Craig K. was hauled onto the carpet in front of "The Man."

He was asked to explain the memo about the accident with the badge and then reads the last line, "I hope the fact that I am a badge collector does not affect the issue." From that day forward, no one ever left that little space after their last paragraph before their signature.

I guess my favourite was when Bob K. was working the Back Room (wiretap lines) covering a Motorcycle President's home conversations. The President gave his wife very strict instructions to ensure there were to be no anchovies on their pizza order. Rumour has it that someone may have called the restaurant and asked to change the order to double anchovies.

The boys then waited and then listened to the very heated domestic occurring in that house for the next few hours. Sucks when you are bored and try to make the best of it.

THEY HATED ME

There was the time people at a funeral wanted to kill me. A young lady had been sunbathing in her backyard one hot summer's afternoon. Her house was on Leslie Street just south of Dundas Street East in #55 Division. She was found there later in the day and had been sexually assaulted and murdered. The Homicide Squad identified as a possible suspect a young man living immediately next door.

I was attached to a M.S.S. team, and we set up surveillance on his house a few days after the homicide had occurred. I recall it was another hot summer's day, and on this same day, they were holding the funeral for the young girl. St. Joseph Church was only a few hundred feet south of where she lived on Leslie Street, and the area was packed with mourners. I was parked in my car just south of the church, able to respond if "our guy" exited his house.

As bad luck would have it, he did exit the house at the exact same moment as the funeral procession was just exiting the church lot onto Leslie Street. I pulled out from my position and was slowly driving north on Leslie passing the church. The lead funeral car had just pulled out in front of me and the hearse was next. The streets were lined with very emotional family and friends. I cut off the hearse and split the procession.

People were yelling at me, and the cars behind the hearse were honking their horns. I tried to play the extremely stupid driver, and waved sorry and trying to apologize, all while continuing forward in my car. They wanted my ass! I was now the target of their built-up frustrations, and they hated me.

I was glad I always drove with my doors locked in case someone ever tried to rip me out of my car. I crept forward and finally passed the lead car and joined the team at the corner of Dundas and Leslie. We left the area following our target. I knew they were hot back there, and I was very lucky to get out of that situation alive. It was my bad luck that she was killed on that street, the suspect lived on that street, and the funeral on that street was leaving at that moment.

Inside I was screaming, "I am one of the good guys and am trying to catch the piece of shit that did this to your young girl." I couldn't tell them, and they would never know. After a few days of surveillance, the Homicide Squad charged buddy next door with her murder, and it was all over the news. I still felt bad for adding more anguish to the mourners that afternoon.

THE LEGEND

There was a shoot-out at high noon on Avenue Road. I don't like to tell stories if I was not there, but this one is worth it. Remember, this is the story as I was told it.

Our legend was one particular Hold Up Squad Detective. Now he was a huge man with a short cigar between his teeth and a no-bullshit attitude. There were two men that were casing a high-end jewellery store on Yorkville Avenue. On this Saturday, he had a team from M.S.S. watching the store and the suspect's car parked nearby on Avenue Road. The two men entered the jewellery store and quickly exited a few minutes later.

Just after they entered their car on Avenue Road, our Detective grabbed his shotgun and walked towards the car. Suddenly there was a loud BANG and he immediately fell to the ground.

All the M.S.S. cars leaped forward to the shooting location, and the foot surveillance operatives moved in. Apparently almost all were now raining the car with .38 bullets and shotgun blasts from their short pistol-grip shotguns. The occupants of the car ducked down and sped off. Their newly ventilated car was found in an alley only a few blocks away. Now their car was not Bonnie and Clyde ventilated but rather like junk yard car ventilated. The Detective was trying to get up from the street as another Investigator advised the store had not been robbed. Apparently while the clerk was busy, they reached over and removed the cash from the till. This was only a theft, also known as a "Till Tap." Additionally, when he had approached the suspect's car he tripped, and the shotgun went of accidentally. He had not been shot. To everyone present, it looked like the suspects had shot the Big Man as he approached the car. It was amazing that on a mid-day Saturday, a shoot-out could occur at Avenue Road and Yorkville Avenue and not one other car, window or anything was hit by a stray bullet. I don't know the details of the apprehension, but do believe they were caught. I like to think the two were caught hiding under their bed, shaking, and wondering why the Undercover cops were so pissed off with just a theft! For me, it was a good weekend to be off.

THE BEST THING HE SAID

I realized that not all lawyers are good lawyers. One of the Squads made an urgent call for a surveillance team as their wiretaps had advised them one of their major players was about to attend an important meeting. We located the target and started to follow him. It wasn't too long before he stopped at a bar just off Dundas Street West and entered. I entered the bar and saw our target had met another man, and they were sitting at a table with two drinks.

I seated myself at a table but was not close enough to hear the conversation. Maybe ten minutes later, our guy got up and walked near the door and started to use the pay telephone.

I walked towards the washroom and decided it was too close to use the second phone right beside him. I continued to the washroom and then waited two minutes. As I passed the second time on my way back, I heard him say, "I just made the deal for the gun and we are going to get it now." After finishing my drink, I left the bar to inform the crew, and we stuck around to ID the fellow he had just met. The investigators advised that was all they required, and we dropped our observations.

It was about one year later that I got a call advising I was required immediately in court as a "surprise witness" for the Prosecution. I took the stand in my jeans and T-shirt and gave the evidence as to my observations. I was then cross-examined by the target's defence lawyer. He repeated my statement and seemed "amazed" that I heard those words being spoken by his client. I advised that is what I had heard.

Now this lawyer repeated to me two more times, "Isn't that amazing that is all that you heard! The best thing he had to say and that's what you heard!" I answered each time, "Your Honor, that's what I heard." It was the third time he said the "best thing" comment that I decided to politely shut this bad lawyer down.

I turned away from him and gave the Judge my entire attention and addressed the Court directly calmly stating, "Your Honor, defence counsel keeps asking me how it is I only heard the "best" thing his client said and nothing else. Sir, I can't say this was the "best" thing he had to say, I may have missed something really good, but that's what I heard!"

The entire court broke into a quiet giggle, and the smiling Judge said to the defence lawyer, "Sir, I think you had better move on." The red-faced lawyer had been checkmated and had no more questions of me that day.

DUDE - WHERE'S MY CAR?

During my time in Intelligence, we had a few minutes between plays and met in the parking lot of the LCBO on Gerrard Street East near Pape Avenue. One of our guys had a white folding cane as a prop. He did the blind man act and tapped his way to the centre of the parking lot and spoke to a passing lady. He asked her if there was a maroon Chrysler in the lot. She said there was. He asked her how far it was from them. She told him it was about 20 to 30 feet to his right. He thanked her and started to tap, tap, tap, his cane as he slowly walked away to his right.

His dark sunglasses also gave him that Stevie Wonder look. She watched him and wondered what he was doing. He took his keys out of his pocket, fumbled at the lock and entered the car. He fired it up and drove it out onto Gerrard Street and away. She froze there and tried to assess this happening for some time as the four of us pissed our pants standing off to the side watching this.

The other stunt we did was similar. Our undercover radio was concealed under the driver's seat. We would make sure the volume was loud enough and then parked it in the middle of the lot. We were situated off to the side with our radio on also. As the right subject walked past the car, we would say into our radio "Psst! Hey! Help. I'm locked in the trunk!" I was always happy to open the trunk and show them an empty compartment and watch the perplexed expression on their faces.

KIDNAPPING

There was a kidnapping investigation that meant life or death depending on if we were detected. A former Hamilton area businessman was drinking in a bar in North Bay where he started to chat up a lady he had just met. They were getting along well and made plans to leave together for some more action. Somewhere outside, he was jumped by her associates, as they had planned. Buddy was tied, taped and tossed into the Mafia-size trunk of his big Buick.

The lid was shut, and the kidnapping had begun, as they had planned. Metro Police were advised, and our Intelligence Services commenced an investigation. The Investigators somehow identified one possible suspect that may have some involvement in this crime. The day shift of M.S.S. was given "the clues" and shortly after picked up on this possible suspect. They followed this guy all day long in the St. Jamestown area of #51 Division. He was a non-descriptive, tall white guy in his 30s with dark hair and always carried a black briefcase. The team did an excellent job of foot surveillance and vehicle surveillance, following him as he took several taxi cabs.

I recall around 3 p.m. I was working the afternoon shift, and we headed downtown to relieve the day shift. We brought downtown a whole new fleet of vehicles and surveillance operatives to increase our chances of avoiding detection.

Our team continued to follow this guy, and nothing so far seemed to implicate him in any crime. As the evening progressed, he went from one place to another until he was picked up by an unknown male in a car. He was driven north of Toronto to the Jane Street area of Concord, Ontario. It must have been around 10 p.m. now, and up there at that time, it felt like 2 a.m. and totally deserted. It was difficult to make sense of his movements, but we wanted to see where this ride was taking him. Just east of Jane Street, they pulled into an industrial complex. There were rows of many different companies with a door and window at the front and a loading dock and garage door at the back of each. Now our challenge began.

The vehicle started a purposeful "spin" of this entire complex, without committing to any one specific unit.

We were all stationary in our vehicles "leap frogging" the "eye" on the car without driving. At one point, I had to turn down a rear aisle in my car and quickly park at the back of a unit's garage door. I quickly shut the car and its lights off and laid down on the front floor, avoiding touching the brake pedal. The suspect car had turned down my aisle and slowly passed the rear of my car without stopping. I always had my driver's window down only about half an inch so I could hear the car pass without being required to peek a look for its position. I was in a very vulnerable position and, of course, my gun was in my briefcase on the rear seat out of my reach. Their car could be heard slowly cruising by and around the next corner.

After about 20 minutes of this intentional spin, we were certain this location was worthy of our attention as a possible location of interest. A member of the team could see the drop-off and which exact unit Mr. Briefcase entered. The car then left the area with the driver being the sole occupant. I took up observations on the front doors from a hilltop across the street. Using binoculars and night vision, I watched the front while another member watched the rear garage area. Several hours had passed without any activity, and it looked like he had been dropped off here for the night. The Investigators made a difficult decision to proceed as if our victim was being held inside and Mr. Briefcase was there as the night-time guard.

Arrangements with York Regional Police Service and MTP ETF (Metro Toronto Police Emergency Task Force) were being made for a dynamic entry into this premise. Hours later, I had a front row seat as YRP (York Regional Police) Tactical Unit used a sledge hammer and smashed in the large plate glass front window on top of a sleeping Mr. Briefcase. At the same time, our ETF used a ram truck to smash through the rear garage door. Mr. Briefcase was taken into custody, and the two handguns that he had been carrying inside the briefcase earlier were now removed from his pants belt line. A large Buick was located inside the rear garage, and when the trunk was opened, the gagged and tied-up victim was found inside. He had been left in there for about four days and was alive. They hadn't untied him to feed him, go the bathroom or stretch his muscles. He was now free.

I reflected on it later that, if I had been detected laying in the front of my car, or any other member of the team had been detected at any time during that day, afternoon or night, Mr. Briefcase would have not gone to that Unit and would have just let the guy die there. I give the credit to the professionalism of all the members of M.S.S.

Note: Patrick Vincent Mancini, the North Bay, Ontario, millionaire rescued from a five-day kidnapping ordeal by a 30-man police team equipped with tear gas, owes his freedom to instructions his abductors gave for delivery of a $1 million ransom.

In a daring raid, police from four municipalities surrounded a warehouse in an industrial plaza northwest of Toronto at about 4 a.m.

They rammed a police truck through a barricade to free the 52-year-old real estate developer, who had been held captive in a car trunk for five days.

Charged with kidnapping, conspiracy to kidnap and possession of firearms with intent to commit an indictable offense, were John Machibroda, 52, Louis Allen Molnar, 60, and Elzbietha Mariol Rybak, 24, all of Toronto, and Josef Duszenko, 37, of Montreal.

A SAFE JOB

There was a Project where we worked an old-time B and E (break and enter) guy one weekend. His name was Bill H. and he lived in the Brampton area. He and his old buddies had a reputation as being a senior gang performing safe jobs. One of our investigative units put in a request for M.S.S. to work these guys as they believed they were responsible for a recent safe job. The suspects in this one backed a box van to a concrete wall, opened the back door and smashed a large hole in the wall. This bypassed the alarm systems. They moved the safe to the hole and started to load it into the van when it fell to the ground between the van and the outside wall. We can only visualize their panic as they could not lift the safe from the ground to the van and eventually had to leave it there.

One quiet Saturday, our Team Leader went through the request files. There were no priority Homicide or Hold Up requests at that time, so it was decided to see what old Billy H. was up to. We set up on his high-rise apartment building in Brampton where he lived with his wife. We went into full radio silence in this area as it was believed he might have a scanner in his apartment. We created a series of radio "clicks" to indicate "out of the apartment" and then the direction. No words were spoken all day, while within a few miles of the apartment. A few hours later he popped out in his car with his wife. Click, click…. click.

Once we reached the highway, we all fell into our grouping and followed them using our regular MSS-coded English conversation. They went west and south to the Queen Elizabeth Way Highway out of Toronto and Mississauga.

This turned out to be a good drive and more than we expected. We passed Oakville, Burlington and Hamilton. I think it was Grimsby where they got off the highway. They drove directly to a little Mall in the centre of town and entered. This Mall had maybe two big stores and several smaller businesses, nothing special. She bought some trivial item and, within ten minutes, they were back in the car and driving back home. Report submitted. End of our day.

Maybe a month later, the requestee called our office and asked for a Team to work Billy H. as he had information that the gang was becoming active. We followed him from his apartment again and watched Billy pick up two other associates.

They drove to the back of a small business in the Lakeshore Blvd. West and Park Lawn area. Johnny B. and I worked our way through some bushes at the back and laid out under some cover to watch them with our binoculars. It was mid-day and a good location to watch their activities on foot. They had an old van with two bright gold tinted rear windows. We watched as they wiped down their tools, thermal lance rods and acetylene tanks. We hit the jackpot as this job was about to take us with them very soon. Damn! I just realized that we were laying on a nest of red biting ants and decided to back off from that small hill. I took away my many new bites, and we advised the requestee of our sighting.

They were to join us shortly as our backup. Maybe an hour later, the old boys were all driven back to their homes to rest up for that night's activities. We had no idea of the intended target, but we were ready.

As the early evening arrived, they all regrouped after their afternoon naps and used one car and the van to drive to the main highway. While they were west bound on the QEW, I wanted to thank them for the van's two gold-tinted rear windows. The sun caught them both and we could back off about a half mile with about 20 citizens' "shade" cars between them and our Team. Thanks, boys! It might be a long night, and we were playing them very loose.

Surprise! Surprise! One month later and they took us back to that small Grimsby Mall. We now knew that the first time was a dry run and recon with his wife. What luck we just happened to have worked them on that day.

We were also familiar with this area and the intended target. It was closing time on a Saturday evening, and the two vehicles just parked in the front watching everything. We took positions at the rear and all four corners out of sight and most of us out of our cars. Johnny B. and I were at the rear on the other side of a chain link fence. We were laying in tall grass and covering the entire rear area. Now the old boys were circling the Mall in the truck. On one pass, they dropped their bag of tools on the rear roadway. It was now after dark, and on another pass, they used a .22 calibre rifle to shoot out the rear security lights.

We could hear some other noise back there but didn't know what it was. Apparently, it was the sound of wire cutters on our chain link fence. Shit! They had cut a hole in our fence and were now walking immediately over to Johnny and me. I could hear their footsteps on the cinder pathway and now could see the one guy from the knees up.

We were dressed in dark clothing and had hoods covering our heads, but Johnny had white runners that were picking up the light. I had just mentioned it to him and he wanted to cut off his feet. Luckily, they passed over us and didn't see us. I told Johnny later that if they had seen us, I would have to kiss him, yell in my girly voice, "Run! Security!" and saunter off with my "partner" holding hands. I further advised him that I would then have to kill him. He understood! The guys returned to the rear again on their side of the fence. Game on!

The requestee had spoken to the local police. I believe it was Niagara Regional, and they kept the entire afternoon shift on overtime to standby the area for the take-down. We had total control over the situation and had not been detected. We watched the rear as they made their move. They finally picked a rear door to make their entry inside. It was their plan to enter the Mall and spend the entire weekend using their tools on the businesses' safes. Unfortunately, these losers picked the wrong rear door out of a dozen or so.

The door they had smashed in belonged to a pet store where a man was sleeping for the night as the caretaker for the pets. He was surprised and screamed loud enough that the old boys panicked and ran out. I announced that something had gone down in a bad way and these dudes were fleeing in all directions out the back area. We don't panic, and we knew where their car and van were and covered them both. Our intention was to let them get to the vehicles and take them down where and when we decided in a controlled situation.

Apparently, the group of uniform police officers gathered together heard our communications and said, "F… this! We're moving in now!" They pounced on our area and were lucky they didn't lose these guys. They were in custody eventually and our job was done. This gave the old gang lots to think about in jail and whether they should take up another profession. Click, Click!

THE TORONTO MAFIA

I watched how the Mafia chooses to kill off others. The crime families in Toronto were well established and consisted of Michael Racco, his wild son Domenic, the Commisso family and others like Paul Volpe. Over the years, I was in certain surveillance projects that allowed me to watch these people in action. Many times, we sat outside the Commisso Banquet Hall on Lawrence Avenue West to cover a meeting that was taking place. I was told that once one of our surveillance cars and operative was detected there and then suddenly surrounded and boxed in with many large Italian dump trucks. I recall watching Michael Racco (the Godfather) having meetings on the street in front of his St. Clair Avenue West Bakery. One not to trust the possibility of wiretaps, he would go outside of the business to have a meeting with his associates. I was also involved in several surveillance projects watching the Commisso enforcer and former Satan's Choice member. I will call him Brian. Brian ran a gym in the west end and drove a baby blue Chev Impala.

Members of my unit were following Brian once and caught him doing a break and enter. Unfortunately for him, he was carrying a loaded handgun at the time and was looking at some serious jail time. Brian was also suspected of planting a bomb in a downtown Chinatown restaurant. This was while performing his extortion duties for the Mob.

He planted his device in the middle of the night and sprinted his four blocks to his car. The device went off, and a midnight kitchen staff member was killed in the explosion. He said later that he believed the building was empty during the late-night hour.

A dedicated surveillance team was developed to try and gather evidence against Brian for the homicide. It was during this surveillance that they watched his blue Impala pull into the parking lot of Casa Loma and park. He pulled up beside another vehicle and the two men started to talk. After the meeting, Brian left the area, and the team identified the second car as an unmarked R.C.M.P. vehicle. O.K., why was their subject meeting the R.C.M.P.?

It appears this tough guy was very afraid of going to jail and was trying to make a deal with the R.C.M.P., unknown to Toronto Police Intelligence. He wanted to rat on the Mob and save his own you know what. His crime family had wanted him to kill the girlfriend of a U.S. gangster and Paul Volpe of the Toronto organized crime scene. Brian felt that if he committed these hits, that the Family would then have him killed to cover their tracks.

This now developed into an O.P.P., Toronto Police, R.C.M.P. Joint Intelligence project. Brian was to reveal and confess to all his past crimes and give evidence about each. He was also to set up the Commisso family for the murder conspiracies to obtain full immunity for past crimes plus get $250,000 in cash.

Toronto Police was now losing their break-and-enter case, gun charges and the Chinatown murder to take down the Commisso crime family.

The wheels were set in motion, and I recall sitting on the high ground of a parking lot on Dixon Road watching that sky-blue Impala meeting Commisso and the two talking inside the now "wired" car. Details were discussed about the murder plans, and it was all being recorded. I was taking several surveillance photographs from my car across Dixon Road.

A few days later, arrangements were made in the U.S. to grab and hide the mobster's girlfriend. Paul Volpe was approached by the investigators who told him he was dead as they took him into the R.C.M.P. building on Jarvis Street. He turned over his wallet to have proof of death.

Brian met once more with the Commisso brothers. We followed him as he drove to their house on Ellerslie Avenue just down the road from #32 Division of Toronto Police. Commisso took Brian to the basement bathroom where he turned on the sink's tap to make some background noise. Brian said he had killed Volpe and produced his wallet. He requested payment as he wanted to get out of town. Commisso said he would meet him on Dixon Road later that evening with the money.

We followed Commisso as he drove directly to St. Clair Avenue West and approached the Racco Bakery. I walked by as Domenic Racco and he were having a meeting on the street. I had to cover this but get off the street.

Using my skills, I was quickly inside an apartment and watched the two during this meeting. I wish I had "ears" on that conversation. Here I was watching the two top crime families talking about a hit that they think had just occurred. After about fifteen minutes, they each went their separate ways. We followed Commisso home.

Brian met again on Dixon Road in that blue Impala with Commisso. He was paid and Commisso drove off with several others in his car. After the Commisso vehicle started west bound on the Queen Elizabeth Way, it was stopped and they were arrested. The Commisso brothers were charged and convicted with the conspiracies and got about 6 and 8 years. This was not before they put out a $250,000 death contract on Brian, and the bikers added a zero-dollar contract also.

Paul Volpe was found dead a few years later in the trunk of his wife's BMW at Terminal 2 in Pearson Airport in 1983. No one was ever charged.

Domenic Racco was also murdered in late 1983. He was walked down an abandoned railway line and shot. Four men with mob ties were convicted of his murder.

Brian immediately entered the Witness Protection Program and testified against any biker, associate, gun dealer and mobster he had ever been involved with. I was one of many on his security team and recall later following him on country roads while he practiced sprinting about the distance of four blocks.

LIFE IN THE WITNESS PROTECTION PROGRAM

Without going into too much detail, life was different living with someone the bad guys were after. You adapt and learn how to survive. You never answer a hotel room door without a pillow in front of you and your drawn gun behind it, even after an inspection looking through the keyhole. When you approach your parked vehicle, you must do a visual inspection for explosives hidden underneath. The "bomber" you are protecting will leave his door open when you start the car. He says that way he may survive and be blown out of the car. The "bomber" does not appreciate it if you jump on your seat, point yourself out the open door and point your two closed hands over your head like a diver off the high board. He will know immediately you are making fun of him, and it's not a good thing to piss off the "hitman." Just saying!

You always have your firearm with you, even when you go to the washroom. When playing cards, the top of the table looks like something from the O.K. Corral period with guns lying there beside the cards. Each room will have a shotgun or sniper rifle lying loaded and safety off against the doorway wall frame.

When you attend bars, restaurants and poolside, there will always be a briefcase laying against your right leg. Affectionately given a code name of "Suzie", this was your 9mm Uzi machine pistol.

The weapon was loaded, safety off, set to semi-automatic and two additional magazines in the foam cut-out inside. That's about a hundred rounds of ammunition.

There was only one man in the world that knew where in the country (or in the U.S.) you were. You gave your one chosen family member that R.C.M.P. Sergeant's phone number in case of an emergency. This was prior to cell phones, but regardless, they would be off to prevent tracking. He would be the only person that knew where you were. He would contact you and ensured you called home immediately. That's one reason that only single officers were on this detail. You were totally "out of touch" for at least three days at a time. At all times, you're looking for surveillance being used on you. Therefore, the members on this detail were only experienced surveillance officers. They were well suited to detect any type of surveillance being used on them.

I recall we met many other citizens and sometimes the odd woman while in a late-night bar. My cover story was I was up in the north testing the lakes for acid rain. It worked and usually shut down the conversation, unless you met a marine biologist.

Security was secondary to most of us, and the focus of a lot of our time was in keeping "our guy" busy and occupied. We knew him well and his psychological problems would flare up if he was getting stressed. Those "eyes" would tell us first and then the nervous twitching.

Your eyes were constantly scanning every person and every car for signs of something unusual. This was all being done while acting very discreet and natural in your undercover capacity. The Secret Service make no attempt to hide who they are and what they are doing.

They don't have to as their function is totally different. There were some sightings of us. Don't ever underestimate the Intelligence network within Organized Crime. Lucky for us we were weeks ahead of any sighting and moved frequently to prevent any tracking.

The wife of the R.C.M.P. Sergeant running the project was privy to all the details of her husband's difficulties in dealing with our protected subject. She took advantage of joining her husband one weekend up north to deliver supplies to the team. I had been with "him" out water skiing that morning with some "friends" we had met the night before. I pulled up to meet them at the chosen rendezvous location.

After we arrived, the Sergeant couldn't wait to come up to me and tell me about his wife's anticipation and what had just occurred. When she finally thought she saw him, she said to her husband, "Oh, my God, he does look like a real PUKE!"

Apparently, the Sergeant advised her, "No dear, that's Cunningham!

"Our guy is the one in the passenger seat." It makes you think about your look. Maybe not so bad if you are undercover. I'll take it.

MIAMI VICE

My job also took me to Miami offshore in a Go-Fast cigarette boat. I was attached to the R.C.M.P. National Criminal Intelligence Section (N.C.I.S.) for one year on the Witness Protection Program. Without going into details, we were protecting, I'll call him Brian, who was under several death contracts by the Mafia and the Bikers. We travelled constantly, but their Intelligence was about two weeks behind us with some occasional sightings of our recent locations. The decision was made to leave the country for awhile to let it cool down here.

My R.C.M.P. partner Freddie D. and I drove "Brian" to the Buffalo border and entered the U.S. Customs Office. One of our team members was given our Uzi, sniper rifle, sawed-off shotgun and handguns to return them to Canada.

We were now stripped of all our protection. We were then met by these two U.S. Marshals that looked like Jake and Elwood Blues. They were dressed in dark suits, white shirts and dark ties while Freddie and I were looking like we were ready for a Grateful Dead concert.

After introductions, the five of us were escorted onto a commercial flight where the Marshals had already purchased the tickets. They were packing (armed) so flashing badges got them and us through security checks, and we were boarded by the flight attendant.

The tickets were checked on three occasions, and we were sat in five centre aisle seats. The door had closed just as a lady passenger approached us and said that we were in her seats. We were on the wrong flight! A quick exit and then our plane was the next one to be brought to the same gate. Thank goodness or I'm not sure where we were about to be flown to. Everyone at the gates had misread the tickets they had checked.

Now on our way to New York City, the Dick in me had to say to the Marshals, "You guys are good! To put us on the wrong flight and get us off just before it was about to leave. That's great counter surveillance!" They just smiled, a little embarrassed and not knowing my sick humour. After a three-hour layover in New York, we then flew to Miami. Their protection team met us in vans with the windows blacked out and drove us to one of their safe houses. This was so Brian was not allowed to know where he was to be held. The next day the Marshals dressed down to our casual level. Freddie and I were now just handlers and they did the security. I was not aware that the company was going to send me on this working "vacation".

I had just been to visit friends in Florida a few weeks prior to this during a week I had taken off from this detail. Freddie had never been there before, so I told him to take our off-duty car and screw off to Key West for the week and have fun. No one in Toronto would know, and I would cover for him.

I would just book out of our off-duty hotel and stay in one of the mansion's rooms at the safe house and work 24/7. Freddie grabbed his backpack and drove off west into Monroe County on U.S. 1 to the end of the road for a good time. The Marshals took us around for a great tour of the area, and I had a few good nights with the boys in the bars of old Miami Beach. They were all war veterans and had great stories. Being just Canadian, I felt my high school football stories were not equal to their wartime experiences. I knew I had some pretty good protection.

One day they had a surprise for Brian and me. The local Head Marshal for all the Florida District invited us for a boat ride. He wanted to show off his recently seized drug dealer boat. A few hours later, he was driving us on the biggest, baddest, longest cigarette boat in the shipping channels of the Atlantic Ocean. We were racing around those remote houses on stilts that you've seen on TV. Damn! I could swear I heard Phil Collins singing, and I only needed a white suit and a Ferrari Daytona Spyder. He then wanted to fly us to Key West in his newly seized drug dealer plane. I stupidly declined this offer.

Freddie missed this one, but I could see him dancing on Duval Street in Key West. After more than a week of this hard work, they sent down a replacement, pulled me out and flew me to northern Ontario for another protection mission.

I always looked back and thought about downtown Toronto and Patrol Area 5217. This was prior to the Entertainment District, and on midnights, you were the only person in that downtown area because there were no residents living there. I knew there was more to life, and thank goodness my experiences with the Force took me far beyond the boundaries of that patrol area to see other things. My only hope for the currently serving members is that you, too, may get the opportunities to work outside of your box (Patrol Area 5217) to apply your trade-craft in a more global environment.

Undercover Intelligence Agent 1979-1984

DON'T DO IT!

I went back to my old high school town to arrest a fellow for murder. A group of Jamaican gangbangers had entered a Toronto jewellery store and forced the owner to the basement. Down there they robbed and then murdered him.

The Homicide Squad was assigned the case, and they requested the assistance of M.S.S. to follow the possible suspect(s). A few days later, a team followed these guys all day watching them pick up associates and eventually enter a gun store where they bought .45 caliber and one other type of handgun ammunition. They had rented a car and information was provided; they were going to Montreal for a party and who knows what else. I was on the afternoon shift, and we responded with our fully gassed-up vehicles to relieve the day shift. We followed these five suspects as they drove all over Toronto, and in the early evening, we started our trip to Montreal on Highway 401. We were performing our usual highway follow with the "eye" car staying well back and behind them and then spread out behind was the rest of the team. At the extreme rear was the backup homicide car monitoring our secured frequency. Sometimes it gets hairy back there, and skilled aggressive driving is required. A car must have ticked off the truckers, and I'm sure they used their CB radios to decide to use a rolling block on the highway. Agent Mikey Butler was trying to pass these trucks and keep up with the team, but two trucks were driving side by side, intentionally preventing him from passing.

He then decided to pass them on the right-side at about 70 to 80 mph using the gravel shoulder.

I was calling the movement east of Cobourg and then announced the vehicle was exiting into the

Service Centre just east of Brighton. They pulled up to the pumps, and Detective Steve Duggan of the Homicide Squad called for a quick meeting at the back of the parking lot. It was decided we would take them down right here and now. Tactics and positions were discussed, and we re-entered our cars.

I was now carrying my pistol-grip short shotgun that I always had down the side of my Camaro's seat on all Hold Up and Homicide plays. I staggered the load with Slug, SSG, Slug, SSG. That would let me always eject the first round if the other was more appropriate, given the surroundings at the time. I always recall the Police College video they showed us where Doug Diplock (ETF) shot the SSG into the screen door and suspect. He was thrown back down the hallway and dead before his feet returned to the floor. The pictures showed an eight-pellet pattern the size of your fist in his chest. A slug shot would have put a window in him.

We all rounded the gas station just as Mike Butler pulled up behind the suspects' car and, more than gently, smashed into their rear end while they were still in the car at the pumps. This distraction gave us the few seconds to drive at their car from all directions, exit and approach the vehicle with our weapons drawn.

I went to the driver's side rear door and, with "my little friend", had all three rear seat passengers comply with putting their six hands on the roof liner of the car. Steve Duggan was on my left with his service revolver pointed at the driver. All our guns on both sides were pointed down into the car to prevent a crossfire situation.

Suddenly I heard Steve yell twice, "Don't do it! Don't do it!" I didn't know what "it" was and could not look over to see. We had each other's back, and it was up to him to deal with it.

Apparently, the driver was reaching to retrieve from under his seat his .45 calibre handgun. He saved his own life by stopping his hand and raising both. I would hate to think what would have happened if anyone fired a shot then. We now had control, and all were put onto the pavement, searched and handcuffed. Two loaded handguns were recovered in the car.

A couple of truckers had entered the lot and watched the take-down by the heavily armed undercover cops. When Mike Butler returned to his car, one of the truckers approached him and apologized, saying he didn't know he was an Officer when he blocked the highway. Mikey simply replied saying, "It's O.K., I'm a country boy and am used to driving at high speeds on gravel."

We loaded up the suspects and took them into Brighton to this little old house of an O.P.P. station. I was quite familiar with this little house as I had spent my high school years going to Brighton High just ten years earlier.

I recalled that each year on Halloween, about a hundred of us would collect eggs and every fruit and vegetable possible and have an all-out spirited gang fight on the main street for about three hours. The one and only town cop would hide, and at about 11 p.m., he would come out with one officer from that little old house of an O.PP. station to try and regain their town. This year, a wild piece of fruit or vegetable smashed through the bank window and set off the alarm. The Mayor had to read us the Riot Act for us all to "disperse and return to our places of abode."

So here I am, ten years later, in a small office in that little house, with the Jamaican driver. I had booked him in for murder and was now removing his jewellery and personal effects. I noted everything in my memo book. Steve Duggan came in and told me that the jewellery I had seized from the accused was, in fact, from the robbed store. What an idiot! Here he was wearing this evidence many days later. I thought how Justice had prevailed and of my pending Court Cards.

MY HOME TOWN

There was one other time I returned to my home town while involved in a surveillance project. We were following a major drug trafficker all over Toronto one night when we started driving two hours east on Highway 401. A few hours later, we arrived at a residential address in Trenton, Ontario. It was late in the evening, and a relief was not going to be possible. The subject could leave this address at any time, so we were compelled to stay with him all night until the next day when our relief would arrive from Toronto.

My parents lived in Trenton but had closed up the house and headed to Florida for the winter. I used the hidden key and opened the house for us to use it. My house was only a few blocks from the address the subject was visiting. This would allow us to sleep in beds with our radios beside us and our members watching the house in two-hour shifts. This sure beat sleeping in a car during the winter months.

As part of our protocol, we contacted Trenton Police to advise them of our presence and to supply local information on the address our suspect was visiting. Now to backtrack only ten years, I used to work for Trenton Police. While I was attending Loyalist College, I was hired as their summer station operator between my first and second year as a law student. It was just me and the Staff Sergeant inside with one marked east car and one west car divided by the Trent River.

I answered the phones, dispatched the cars, recorded this on the Unit Commander's Morning Report, and performed Telex duties. These were the times when a passing transient could use an open cell for the night like a hostel. I worked five days a week from 7 p.m. to 3 a.m. with only Sunday and Monday off for the three summer months. It was a valuable experience, and what else was there for an 18-year-old to do?

Now I was returning as an undercover Intelligence Officer with Metro Police. I met their Detective and advised him of our investigation. He remembered me from my time there before, and he did recognize this long-haired plainclothesman. He didn't have anything to offer on our target address but understood we were going to be there for some time. I had the Detective in my car cruising the address and then downtown while we talked. The full team was still on the road now and locked on our address. In a few hours, we would scale back to the night mode and open my house as our own personal hostel.

As we were cruising downtown in my car, the Detective interrupted and said "Hey, there's one of our most active subjects." He was referring to a car ahead of us that contained some local character they had been involved with. I thought we were available and our entire resources (except one car on our target house) could be available to "spin' this local dude and maybe catch him in the act of something the Detective could use. I thought it might be fun, and there was no way Trenton Police would ever have the opportunity to utilize the service of a full surveillance unit.

We were ready to give this guy a spin locally and see what may happen. The vehicle pulled up to the light in front of the town cinema, and I pulled in the lane beside it at the light. I ensured I stopped just short of the right passenger window in the driver's blind spot. I looked straight ahead to avoid any eye contact with the subject when "IT" happened!

This small-town Detective pulled a Barney Fife! While we were stopped at the light, he decided to lean forward in his seat, look past me and directly at the driver, and once he had purposely obtained eye contact with him, he waved at the driver. I could hear a "howdy" in there, even though nothing was said. I could also hear, "Hey, look at me and where I am and I'm watching you." O.K., game over! I pulled off and dumped his ass back at his little stone house of a police station.

He had the full resources of the most elite surveillance unit of a municipal police force in all of Canada. He blew the opportunity, and I had expected more. The team kept their "eye" all night long on our drug address and got a decent night's sleep.

In the morning, our relief arrived from Toronto and we headed back. During our drive back, I appreciated the world that I now lived in and re-instated the fact I could never return to policing in a small town or city. Policing in Trenton, Belleville, Peterborough, or anywhere but Toronto would mean a long 30 years and the lack of opportunities and challenges my new city offered and I needed.

THE SPORTING LIFE

The Police were being offered deals at Sporting Life. Apparently, a good citizen noticed two suspicious men in a car watching the Sporting Life store on Yonge Street in #53 Division. The Hold Up Squad was assigned to investigate them, and they requested assistance from M.S.S. Sure enough, the team observed the pair as they watched the closing of the store for several nights during the week. They would observe the manager close the store and, with his wife, take the night deposit a mile south to their apartment in the Yonge and Chaplin Crescent area. He would drive his BMW into their underground garage and then take the elevator to his apartment.

The team now photographed and identified the two but never knew which night they might proceed with their plan. With the absence of any informants or wiretaps, we didn't have a conspiracy charge.

Friday night came and went, and it was another dry run. The team was so disappointed as they were scheduled to be off the weekend and they wanted to see this to its conclusion. My team was on for the weekend, and we studied their notes and photographs. Early Saturday, we locked on these guys and spent the whole day at the gym and driving after them all over Toronto. As the evening approached, they assumed their position across the street in the lot watching the store. Our money was on them that this was the night!

The Hold Up Squad used our surveillance van and was positioned in the underground garage. They were going to jump these guys outside of the elevators.

Mr. Manager and his wife entered their BMW with the cash and drove home. The bandits followed them, and we followed the bandits. The manager had not been clued in and was unaware of the whole situation. Now Murphy's Law kicked in. For the first time, the manager didn't drive into the underground garage. Rather, he pulled up to the front door at the circular drive and left his wife in the car as he entered the building. The HUS (Hold Up Squad) had been monitoring our radio conversation and kept asking us where the BMW was. The bandits quickly followed the manager into the building. A few minutes later, they exited and drove away with us following. An investigator from the van was sent to the manager's floor to see what had occurred. We continued to follow the car and waited for the word to get back to us.

Apparently, when the investigator was on the right floor, the manager could be heard screaming for help. He was in his apartment handcuffed to the toilet. He advised that he had been robbed. He was so pleased that a "passing citizen" had heard his screams for help. We were now given the word that there had been a robbery and the manager was O.K.

I recall being hung at a traffic light beside the suspect's car and casually glancing over at these two men. I saw that they were stone-faced, looking straight ahead, not talking, and at one point the passenger wiped sweat from his forehead.

There were no celebrations or high fives, nor were they looking back or around for a tail.

This was a great opportunity for me as I always tried to study people in all situations. Now it was just a matter of picking the right time and place to do a hard take-down. We usually liked Black Creek Drive in case shots were fired, but we were not near there. The Hold Up Squad caught up and they were taken down without incident near their home address. It was my understanding that we could get a nice discount for sporting goods after that, but I never checked it out.

Undercover Intelligence Agent 1979-1984

MORE THAN YOU ASK FOR

Sometimes when you are spying on someone, you get more than you ask for. I recalled when we were requested to follow a man and the details of why eluded me. I do though recall certain other aspects of that day.

The surveillance unit set up on his home in the west end - Albion Road area. The street he lived on was a residential street and a crescent. Due to the curve of the road it was difficult to get a direct "eye" on the front of his house. We were required to use two cars to cover each end of his street that dumped out onto the main street. He could leave after a pickup and we would miss it, but we stayed in position. I would always strive to find a better eye, regardless of the difficulties if it was the right thing to do. After a few hours, I looked for a better eye and located one. There was a five-story Senior's Retirement Residence a short distance east of our target street. I approached the building super, and a few minutes later, I was on the rooftop of this building. I advised the team I had a better eye to cover the street and entire block. I could see any arrivals and departures from our target home.

Of course, I had taken my cheaters (binoculars) up there with me, and for the next few hours, I had direct vision on the entire neighbourhood. This was not the most exciting task and, like surveillance, it is hours of boredom followed by minutes of excitement once the target moves.

When I was in the surveillance mode, nothing moved in my field of vision without this spy catching it. I was drawn to some movement a few homes from our target house. There was some activity inside another residential home clearly visible through its large sliding glass doors. While maintaining my task of our target house, I was also able to multitask. Our training kicks in during stressful times.

There was a lady in her mid-30s wiping down the inside of her glass doors with a rag and window cleaner. It wasn't hard to observe she was totally naked except for a pair of fire engine red bikini panties. The lady was well endowed and very dedicated to her housework. Trying to watch our house became a little challenging, but I hung in there like a true professional. She continued her cleaning and was now vacuuming the dining room area in the same manner. My elevated view allowed anyone on that side of the building above the second floor to look down into her house and over the small "L" shaped wooden privacy fence outside the sliding doors.

I was shocked when she now slid open the door and stood outside on her patio wiping down the outside of the glass doors. Yes, she was standing behind the fence, but it wasn't private anymore to those in my building. This Molly Maid stuff went on for about twenty minutes, but she was doing a very thorough job.

Oh, yes, no movement at our target house. She went inside, and her last act was to shake out her mop through the open doors. Her shaking was also very thorough, and I can report there was no dust left on that mop. After strutting around her dining room for a few more minutes, she seemed to retreat to the deep inside of her house.

Like a police dog too long on the scent, I felt I needed a break and requested a relief. BK came up and caught the last act of the show, and I left. Oh, yes, no movement on our target house. Funny, I can't recall why we were there that day but do recall the sideshow events.

I thought about this later that maybe the boys in the retirement home (upper floors, west side) probably knew what time and day of the week to leave their Bingo game or wolf down their Weetabix to quietly retire to their rooms to read or rest themselves. I also thought that the local Canadian Tire store was probably sold out of "cheaters". I'm not fast but also felt that some hot lady in red knew exactly what she was doing and enjoyed the show. She was very community minded. I hope there was a defibrillator on those floors.

Oh, yes, no movement at our target house.

BAD APPLES

I never would have thought that a theft investigation might be one of the most challenging of all the offences possible.

There was a reason we were isolated from the general police population. One reason was the fact that occasionally we would be required to work a very confidential Internal Affairs project. We all agree that no resources should be spared to remove bad apples, and sometimes these investigations did clear some wrongfully accused officers.

I recalled working a project several times and there was not enough evidence to prove the allegation, but we suspected it was there. Two Toronto Police Officers were married to two east coast sisters. The sisters, and the rest of the family, was known to be involved in Organized Retail Crime and would steal things like sheets and pants to order for their clients. The question was, "Did either or both Police husbands know the source of the money their wives were bringing home?" During two different projects, we followed them and watched the sisters steal lots of stock from the stores, while their brother watched over them. Myself and one of my operatives had to be cautious because we both knew one of the coppers. Maybe eight years earlier, we were Cadets together, and I rented his parents' summer cottage for a week one year. This meant that when I was following him, I could not do foot surveillance and ensured I never got close to his car when he was hung at a traffic light. Other than that, I followed him from my car everywhere he went. The team could always prove the family was stealing from the stores, but the investigation never showed the officers were present or had direct knowledge.

It was approximately one year later we were advised to commence following them again. This time we had a CI (Confidential Informant). It seems a fellow Police Officer worked with these guys and thought it was very suspicious when one of them kept offering him a chance to buy cheap clothing. Our Informant officially approached someone, and Internal Affairs re-opened their investigation. He was told to go ahead and place an order with this fellow officer and we would do the rest.

We started following the family, and sure enough, they were stealing thousands of dollars of products daily. With their brother watching them inside the store, we were required to also enter the store and personally watch them as they stole their items. Now the brother and the two sisters were watching, so there were many eyes on us. We had to act cool, blend in as other shoppers and get the required observations. This was not easy, but we did it and saw it all. The bags went in empty and dropped to the floor. We saw the hands stuffing them from under the stock racks and then leaving with them full. They even lifted their baby in the stroller and stacked maybe 6 packages of linen under the kid. It was so high that he fell off the stack as they rolled him out the door.

As part of our investigation, one of the lead Detectives, Bob Dunstan, entered their car and secretly marked his initials and badge number on the stolen stock. This was while they were making return trips into the same stores. This went on for several days and we were never detected, and the teams performed some excellent surveillance under some very difficult situations. The Crown Attorney's Office was involved, and we had approval to let the thefts occur without an immediate apprehension. Our Informant met the fellow officer in a parking lot one evening while we video-taped the meeting. The clothing was now delivered, and it later showed Detective Bob Dunstan's secret markings.

Internal Affairs arrested the Police Officer and, rather than perhaps go to jail, he agreed to resign immediately. There was never any evidence to implicate the second married officer, but I'm sure he got the message.

The Confidential Informant was immediately transferred out of uniform duties and joined us in the Intelligence Bureau where he remained for most of his career. This brave man had the utmost integrity, and his actions allowed us to close this case once and for all. It would not have been possible without his dedication and professionalism.

Even though I had known this subject Officer, I was happy to be part of removing this bad apple from our service.

THE ACCIDENT

One advantage of working in a specialized unit was, it allowed for the opportunity to attend night school. I did attend George Brown College one evening a week to take Organizational Management and Supervisory Principles courses. It was on one of those evenings I was off duty and returning from class to Richmond Hill when it happened. I had just passed through the intersection of Bathurst and Major Mackenzie Road when two cars met in the intersection. I heard the loud bang and then saw the large fireball in the air from the explosion. An east-bound car had impacted with a west-bound car that was turning south in the intersection.

The accident was just behind me but the 10 p.m. evening sky lit up as the 50-foot high fireball turned the inside of my car into daylight. I immediately pulled the hand brake on my little VW Rabbit and did a "J" turn to return to the corner. The east-bound car was about 50 feet east of the corner and into the side guard rail. My attention was to the car in the centre of the intersection fully engulfed by flames. A young man who had also witnessed the collision stood beside me now, and we looked at a human figure seated in the burning driver's seat. The flames prevented us from getting within 10 feet of the car, and we were unable to tell the sex of the driver. The driver was slumped over the wheel and not moving as the fire raged on.

The young man (later known to me as Rob) and I tried several times to get to the door handle but were not successful. It was a helpless situation for us, and we knew what had just happened. I then ran over to the second car. The entire front end of the car was pushed back and both doors were damaged. The driver had staggered out of the car and was collapsed over the guardrail at the rear of the car. I could see he had head and facial injuries and, I suspected, also internal damage. He was conscious, and I had Rob stay with him while I left for the car. Inside the front passenger seat was a second man, and he was moaning and coming out of unconsciousness. He had facial injuries and I suspected internal injuries also.

That's when I saw "it" and was shocked! On the floor of the driver's side, a radio had slid out from under the seat and was in clear view. I immediately recognized this as an undercover

M.S.S. (Mobile Support Services - Intelligence) radio.

This was an undercover M.S.S. car with two plainclothes Intelligence Officers. I now recognized them both.

Approximately one year earlier, York Regional Police Services decided to start an Intelligence Unit and they sent their officers to our Toronto M.S.S. unit for surveillance training. These men were riding with us for several months on our projects to learn their new jobs. These two officers had worked in my unit many months earlier. I now recognized them both. The police station and fire hall were only a few blocks east of us, and I could hear them coming.

The first YRPS (York Regional Police Service) marked police car arrived, and I approached the young driver. I identified myself and told him he had a Departmental Fatality Accident and to notify his Supervisor and Traffic Unit immediately. I explained to him that the driver of the car burning in the intersection was obviously deceased and the two plainclothes Intelligence Officers has serious injuries and required an immediate run to the nearby hospital.

Rob and I now stood back and let the responding units do their tasks. We once stated how bad we felt about not being able to get to the driver. I went home and, a few weeks later, was contacted by two YRPS Detectives. They showed me a picture of the driver who was a single lady school teacher in her 30s. It was such a nice picture and so sad to recall her ending. I could not advise as to the speed of the police car or the turn by the lady driver as I had passed the corner prior to the accident. The severity of the impact was obvious, and the resulting damage showed it. I do not believe any charges were laid and I was never contacted again.

Maybe 12 months later, I had moved to another location within Richmond Hill and noted one of my new neighbours was the young man Rob from the accident. We became good friends over the years, and to this day, maybe 35 years later, we are still in contact.

In our life experiences, we have flown in his planes, sailed in the Virgin Islands and shared a stock car to name just a few things. We have never discussed the car accident and our feelings in those years that followed.

I guess we felt it wouldn't change a thing.

A HOME OF OUR OWN

We turned a police station parking lot into a furniture display that Leon's Furniture store would have been proud of.

Our M.S.S. project was a City Hall cleaner that was suspected of stealing money from their safe. Coincidentally, he had quit his job and was planning on moving back to New Brunswick.

We started the afternoon shift around 3 p.m. and headed straight to his Scarborough apartment building. In the lot was the large U-Haul moving truck that he and his family were loading with all their possessions. This continued until about 11 p.m. when the team left just two cars there for the over-nighter. BK and I were staying in case he moved during the night. If he was still there in the daytime, the day shift would relieve us.

I have done all-night plays before, and sleeping in the car for a few winks is O.K. as your other car will radio you if there is any movement.

On one other occasion, I was doing one of these, and I was, in of all places, trying to catch a few Zs in the back seat of my Camaro. Mr. Uniform Policeman on patrol caught me as I had kept the engine running to stay warm. After I flashed my Tin (badge), he left and must have wondered why it was O.K. to sleep while working.

Back to the U-Haul van: We had fully gassed cars and were ready for a long night. I think it must have been 3 or 4 a.m. when the guy, his wife and small child entered the truck and started heading east. I have family in New Brunswick and was looking forward to a possible visit and bringing back a dozen fresh lobsters.

We radioed (pre-cell phones) the solo midnight-man back in our office, and we all knew there would be no relief. In about 30 to 60 minutes, we would be out of radio range with the office. We still had a Province-wide shared Intelligence frequency, if we needed it. Each communications unit in all of Ontario monitors this open channel should any Intelligence Agent need to communicate outside of their City.

I was comfortable with it, being in just a two-man surveillance. I had been trained by BK and we worked well together. I know we could have followed this guy the whole way without detection, as we were competent professionals.

Fortunate for us, our Team Supervisor had taken his company car home to Pickering for the night from the project earlier. The office woke him up, and he jumped out of bed and became mobile. I think he drove at Warp 5 and caught up to us past Port Hope on the 401. In those days, speedometers during surveillance were irrelevant.

We now did our three-car follow passing Belleville, Kingston, and the Thousand Islands. An executive decision was made to take this guy down while still in Ontario. The Intelligence channel was used to get an O.P.P. unit to pull over the truck on the 401. The family and the truck were transported to the Brockville O.P.P. station for the investigation. While he was being questioned by our Supervisor, BK and I were detailed to search the contents of the moving van. There was a shit-load of furniture and possessions in this truck, and we were now into mid-day and getting very tired.

This O.P.P. detachment was another one of those little old houses they used to use in the smaller locations. We were in the back lot surrounded by marked police cars within view of the 401 Highway. I recall BK and I were getting giddy and couldn't stop seeing the humour in anything as we were punch-drunk. We carried on with our search mission, but our way!

We grabbed the rolled-up carpet first and opened it fully in the middle of this Detachment's parking lot. Next came the bedroom set including dresser. We complimented our decor with a lamp on a stand and a large living room chair. The couch was placed in the living room area of our fake apartment.

The rooms were all separated and spaced out accordingly. The only thing missing were the imaginary walls. Now anyone driving west-bound on Highway 401 would see a fully furnished open air apartment in the centre of a Police station parking lot and wonder WTF!

The final touch was BK and I seating ourselves on this furniture as we were tired, and it looked so inviting. There was a lot more in the truck to search, but our batteries were low, and we needed a coffee break. It was a nice hot summer's day.

It was now that an on-duty O.P.P. cruiser with a sharp-looking uniformed officer pulled into his parking lot. He stopped well short of the lot when he realized that he was driving into our personal outdoor apartment space. The cruiser was parked just outside our bedroom area. He stared at the two long-haired "pukes" that were sitting on the couch and chair. Without saying anything other than "Good Day" to us, he very slowly entered his station. We got our second wind and were about to tackle all the other items in the truck when we were told buddy had just admitted to the theft and advised of the money's location. We reloaded the truck and finished in the early evening. All three surveillance cars were on auto pilot at about 100 mph all the way home. If nothing else, we were all ace drivers.

We took our cars home that night to save us some more hard time. I think the record stood for many years after that. We had racked up 21 hours of overtime after working an 8-hour shift. Also, I'm certain the tales of these crazy Toronto coppers were repeated there for years after that. No lobster for Hal.

BANKING ON IT

It was a rare opportunity to be present when a bank robbery was in progress.

The HUS (Hold Up Squad) had a group of bandits that they suspected were about to commit a daytime bank robbery in Toronto. These were local guys, and without any "finks" (informants) or wiretaps, we didn't know where and when this was to occur.

My surveillance team was following these guys all over Toronto and, not knowing for sure when or where, made it very challenging. We had to assume they would be looking for surveillance if they were about to rob a bank. That put extra pressure on us: to ensure we followed them very loosely to avoid detection and not lose them.

There were three bandits in this car, and we didn't know much about them. Mid-day they drove north on Leslie Street from Sheppard Avenue East. They made a right turn at Nymark Avenue. At this corner was small plaza with several stores, including a Bank of Montreal in the center of the structure. It was #4751 Leslie Street.

They turned onto the side street behind it, Corning Road, and parked at the rear of this plaza.

John B. had observations on the car at the rear, and I positioned myself in front of the Bank of Montreal. I ensured that I parked facing away from the bank and used my rear-view mirror to cover the front area.

It was quickly identified that there was an open walkway leading from the rear on the Corning Road side running directly west to the front of the bank. Is this the place? Are they about to do a robbery? Can/should we stop it? The HUS was monitoring our conversation, and that decision would be theirs. We just had to be ready to jump out, if required. The other team members covered the side-streets north and south of the car and the main streets to ensure we would be able to follow them as they left the area.

The three men exited the vehicle and John had advised us they were entering the walkway. They were out of sight for maybe ten seconds when I had observations on them as they exited the west end of the walkway at the corner of the bank. I advised the Team and the HUS.

In doing years of surveillance, one thing all operatives learn is to stay calm and especially in your voice demeanor. I went on to stress that in my classes for the next 25 years of teaching surveillance techniques. If you stay calm and professional, your "in control" voice tone will instill a sense of calm and professionalism to all. If you raise your voice and get excited, everyone will increase their excitement and feel you have lost control of the situation.

John B. had calmly, and in detail, described what he saw at the rear and then their direction until they were out of his sight. He then maintained observations on the unoccupied car, as required.

From the vantage point of my car at the front of the bank, I calmly said the following, "O.K., I've got them. They are exiting the walkway and are at the corner of the bank. The three are now walking together south-bound passing the front window of the bank. I can see them looking inside the window as they are walking past it." No one else is talking, and the radio is purposely not used by anyone other than the person on the "eye" calling it. "They have passed the bank and now are standing in front of the convenience store just south of it. The three are now talking to each other. O.K., guys, they have just entered the bank! They are pulling masks over their faces, they have drawn their handguns and two just jumped over the counter."

The HUS backup car came on the air briefly now and instructed us to stay out of the back and let it happen. That was the proper and safest decision for the patrons and staff inside the bank. We couldn't stop it, and entering the bank would only lead to a very dangerous situation for all. They let me continue with the calling.

"It looks like they are done and getting ready to exit. O.K., they are now out of the bank and running towards the walkway. John, are you still there?" John was still at the back and was ready. The take-down would not be here, rather the choosing of the place and time would be made by us and a surprise. "They have turned east into the walkway and are out of my sight now!"

About three seconds later, John came on the air and advised, "O.K., I've got them running to the car and they are all on board." This was all done in a clear, calm, low-tone voice, and we were in total control.

No police cars had been alerted to this due to the quickness of it, and it took no more than five minutes from start to finish. We followed the car away from the area, and they had no idea that they were being followed. You can tell by watching the actions of the car and the heads of the occupants in the car. They had no idea!

Some long distance away, the HUS picked a safe and quiet location for the takedown, in case we were forced into a shoot-out. We boxed them in and did a hard takedown and they didn't have a chance. They were bagged and tagged and off to jail. Everyone was safe, and it was indeed a rush to be in a front row seat and watch a bank robbery in progress.

Undercover Intelligence Agent # 34 - 1979-1984

MY PERSONAL EVEREST

     I consider this my Personal Everest. In the 1970s and 1980s, there was an unwritten rule to the Montreal hold-up gangs from the Metro Toronto Police Hold Up Squad (HUS): "Stay out of Toronto or you might not make it back home!" This was respected by almost all those bad boys as they didn't want to take on this tougher gang.

     I was working in MSS in January of 1984 when our HUS received information that a gang from Montreal was planning a hold-up in Toronto and were about to arrive by train. My surveillance team rushed to Union Station and picked off three men arriving on the train and entering the lower level of the Royal York Hotel.

This was a chap by the name of Fernand Robillard (Mr. R.) and two of his associates. Mr. R. loaded their suitcases into a locker and went towards the Bank in the lower level. Mr. R. entered alone, and I followed. I could be close enough to hear his transaction with the Manager. He was using an alias to try and cash a cheque for $500. I could see the identification he was using and the name and address he offered. After cashing this cheque, I identified myself to the Manager and advised him to hold it as the HUS would be contacting him. Mr. R. and his two buddies then walked 100 feet apart from each other all the way to the downtown Holiday Inn behind the new City Hall. They were obviously checking for surveillance.

Over the next few days, and again several times during January and February, the three would arrive by train and do the same procedure of walking to a different hotel each night and watching for any tails they might have.

All the resources of MSS were assigned to this case. All the teams performed some of the best foot surveillance ever required for many days on end. Vic Dybenko was always in the adjoining hotel room listening to our room probes to translate their conversations for us from French to English. I followed this gang in train stations, underground concourses, streets, hotels, bars and many banks during this time, along with many other surveillance operatives.

I watched Mr. R. and one of his associates case banks in the Queen/Bay and York/Adelaide areas. I watched the two of them check out thoroughly the National Bank building at Adelaide and York Streets. After checking out the inside separately, they met on the corner and had a very heated hand-waving discussion. It appeared to be about the exterior of the bank and that corner and it lasted about ten minutes. They finally left that corner and walked to Church and Wellington Streets, but something had happened! They were now more looking behind them than in front. We had taken some "Heat", meaning we had been detected. There were six cars stopped at the light, and Mr. R. pointed at one of them and his partner walked beside it and checked it out.

One of my fellow operatives was driving this undercover surveillance car, and they were locked on it. They watched it drive away when the light turned green. They now continued to look at everything, so we immediately stopped our observations and left. Vic told us they argued in their room that one of them was sure they were being followed, while the other did not.

Thus, we let the associate go on his test walk alone without us following. After he returned, he said to Mr. R. (in French of course), "You're right! No one is following us!" We were BACK in the game. Thanks, Vic!

Our Intelligence now identified their plan. Their guns, masks, and bulletproof vests were in the suitcase we saw earlier. This suitcase was now inside their room. They had arranged a 7 a.m. wake-up call at the hotel, and then all three would walk separately to the area of the National Bank, shoot the armoured car guard when he arrived, and steal his loot. The morning of the wake-up call, we had three surveillance teams (one for each suspect). We had our instructions from the HUS. Each team would follow a suspect and when out of ear-shot of the others, take him down. If there was any resistance, let's say a criminal proceeding would probably not be required. It was body armour under the street clothes for us all and my pistol grip shotgun under my right armpit for me. We set up much prior to their wake-up call, while they were still napping.

At the last minute, a Senior Officer overruled the HUS plan and had the ETF blow a hole in their hotel room door. Using tear gas, they then dragged their naked bodies into the hallway with assault rifles to their heads.

I was impacted by Homicide Squad Detective Rob Montrose's lecture years earlier about the "arrest" and how it is full of congratulations. He emphasized that the case does not end there. He stressed this is only the beginning with the need for detailed notes, proper case preparation and detailed evidence being presented on the stand to back everything up. I always took testimony on the stand seriously and studied good, and, yes, also bad, testimony in court all the time. I followed and studied the Oliver North hearings and the O.J Simpson trials religiously from an evidence/testimony perspective.

Senior Crown Attorney Robert ASH was assigned this HUS case at a bilingual trial. We had worked together a few months earlier on a Toronto Armenian Terrorists case where I gave detailed surveillance observations of the accused. In this Mr. R. case, I, along with many other surveillance operatives, gave many hours of evidence at the Preliminary Hearing in the Old City Hall. Mr. Ash was now ready for the High Court trial in front of the jury.

He advised me I would be the first witness for the prosecution, as I had probably the most observations over the longest period. He started the evidence by calling me to the stand, and immediately I was asked about my surveillance credentials.

He had me qualify and declared, probably the first time in Canada, as an Expert Witness in Surveillance and Counter Surveillance Evidence. The Defence cut him off and agreed, not wanting the jury to hear any more of my experience and qualifications.

Now, this could have been any one of my associates as we all had the same daily experience in the field, but Mr. Ash made the call. For two full days in front of the jury, I went over my evidence of two months of following these three all over downtown Toronto on foot.

I watched the accused Mr. R.'s reaction as I related how I followed him into banks, bars, streets, hotels, elevators and hallways. He now listened, as did the jury, as to how I overheard conversations he had, rode elevators with him, followed him to get his exact room number, listened to him at the bar talking to the waitress, and many other up-close encounters. I could see in his face, "What the F...K! How come I never noticed this guy?"

Believe me, we have never worked a more counter-surveillance target than this group, and the entire office did an excellent job, as the professionals they all are. I can only say that, after many years at this task, we were all groomed to be the King with no clothes on, that no one will ever notice. It is a personal mental state that you acquire and then can pass the target dozens of times in a day. Just change your dress, demeanour, and actions so you are someone no one will ever notice, "Average!"

After my Examination in Chief, and as now an Expert Witness, I could go over my evidence a second time now, giving my opinion as to how they were the most counter-surveillance group we had ever encountered. I then threw in my jargon of "Spin, Heat and Hinky" and could offer my own definitions of each.

Mr. Ash and I utilized this technique at the Armenian Terrorist trial, and it proved to be devastating to the Defence. I used slight demonstrative hand gestures in my testimony to the jury, and at one point, I knew I had them in the palm of my hand.

It was intense, and I was always three or four moves ahead of the questions in my mind.

The jury was made to feel that they were part of this surveillance and could visualize each observation. I left after my two days, and the case proceeded with all the other evidence being submitted. Mr. R. and his buddies were all sent to Collins Bay. I thought I had heard that they were also convicted of about 30 other bank robberies across Canada.

Mr. Ash went on the write a book called A GUIDE TO EXPERT SURVEILLANCE EVIDENCE. It contained his Editorial Notes within a complete transcript of my testimony in front of the jury. He had it distributed to all Crown Attorneys and Surveillance Offices in Canada.

About a year later, I was assigned to #52 Division C.I.B. (Criminal Investigative Bureau). I had heard Mr. R. had successfully escaped from Collins Bay by hiding in the back of a garbage truck.

He should have been crushed to death there as it compressed the garbage with hydraulics each time it stopped. His luck didn't last too long as he was arrested a few months later while shoplifting and packing a handgun. Our HUS then returned him to Toronto and walked him into my CIB.

There were about ten of us Investigators in the room when he was escorted towards the Interview Room with his hands handcuffed in front of him. I sat at my desk as he entered the room. Mr. R. scanned the room with his eyes and then stopped and looked directly at me.

Like the lion cub you grew up with and reunited with many years later, he reacted and lifted his handcuffed hands and pointed and nodded his head several times at me. I had been "Burnt" (detected). I like to think he felt, "Oh, shit! There's that guy again. Is he still following me?"

Bottom line, "Stay out of Toronto!" Signed: TPS HUS

My days of active surveillance work were now completed.

Notes given by Senior Crown Attorney Robert ASH:

"Fernand Robillard was a highly professional criminal and bank robber. His reputation was such that he would advise others on the best techniques for bank robberies. He participated in a string of heists across Canada and was eventually apprehended by the Toronto Police Hold Up Squad. They were able to link him to a whole series of bank hold-ups in the GTA (Greater Toronto Area). Surveillance evidence played a large role in his downfall. An entire book could be written on this man's criminal career. Two trials were required to convict him on many robbery counts. His Appeal to the Supreme Court of Canada was unsuccessful. There were so many Quebec bank robbers coming to Toronto at that time that I felt like the little Dutch boy with his finger in the dam. Robillard got a huge prison term and things quieted down somewhat after his sentencing, thanks to Judge H. Ward and Judge Hector Soubliere. As I recall, Robillard got a sentence in excess of thirty years."

CHAPTER THREE

RETURNING TO UNIFORM/CIB DUTIES AFTER INTELLIGENCE. (1984-1987)
No. 52 Division. (Uniform and Criminal Investigative Bureau) - Constable

BACK TO UNIFORM

I had requested a return to #52 Division Uniform work after five years in Intelligence. I missed the streets and loved the game with the opportunity to enjoy the satisfaction of personally catching the Big One. Often in Intelligence, the final take-down was up to others (Tactical Unit, Requestee). A very positive thing from those many undercover years of watching the Mafia, robbers, bikers, druggies, etc. was it sharpened all five of your senses like never before. One of my former MSS associates said it best: "MSS is not for everyone. It took me a good 18 months until I was able to truly be a policeman, without being a policeman!"

I was working my favourite, the midnight shift with PC Tommy Corbett. We hadn't worked together before, but I knew he was a seasoned veteran who spoke his mind freely and owned the streets. Tommy was driving and was the senior officer on this taxi-cab yellow scout car assigned to a very busy all-night Yonge Street.

It was around 2 or 3 a.m. when the dispatcher said, "Go ahead with the Hotshot, Gasworks, Dundonald and Yonge Street, armed robbery just occurred, suspect last seen south-bound on foot, no description." There were lots of cars clear that would be responding, and because we were east-bound on College Street near Bay, I suggested we check Carlton Street. I felt some cars might wrongly head too close to the scene. Carlton Street was five city blocks south of the Bar.

As we crossed Yonge Street, I noticed a chap running out of the laneway east of Yonge on Carlton. Now this guy was a jogger. It was a hot summer's night, and he was wearing a proper jogging shirt, track pants, sport socks and running shoes. He was jogging at a proper jogging pace, not at an escape run nor wearing Felony Flyers (criminal runners). It all looked so normal, but I still pointed him out to Tom and asked him to stop our car. I exited the police vehicle, looked at the jogger, and he clearly heard the loud SNAP of my front opening clam-shell style security holster. With my firearm at my side, he looked surprised as I instructed him to put his hands on my trunk while I searched him. After holstering my weapon, I had my right hand on his right arm and searched his shirt and pants with a quick pat-down.

He now advised that he lived in the area and was out for his regular evening run. He supplied his name and address and appeared calm. A passing scout car stopped in the middle of the road to watch us, and then they seemed to know this guy. The Officer driving told me he personally knew this fellow who lived at the bottom of the Division, and everything seemed to match what he had told us.

I was now satisfied and said to him, "We have had a hold-up in the area, and you may get stopped and questioned again while jogging, so be cool and don't unduly alarm any officer approaching you." I re-entered our police car and Tom started to drive off.

I can't understand or explain what happened next. We had only moved a few hundred feet in front of Maple Leaf Gardens, and I firmly said to Tom, "Stop! Go back!" Now this poor jogger approached our car for the second time, and again I told him to come to me, and then this time I handcuffed him. I placed him in the rear seat behind the cage. Tom's face showed a total misunderstanding of the events, as did the jogger's. I went to the privacy of outside the scout car and tried to explain myself to my partner. I said this jogger didn't feel right and didn't smell right to me.

As we drove off the first time, my personal computer (my brain) was processing the street encounter. I realized that my right hand, while on his arm, noticed his temperature was not what I would have expected from a jogger. Also, the smell of his sweat was not compatible to my expectations. Bottom line, my Woman's Intuition said to me that this was not right. I went with my gut and said he was going to the station.

As we had just arrived at the station in the Detective Office, I was trying to decide how I would explain this one when we were told they found a black balaclava. It was in the laneway he had exited, inside a garbage can, and it had a long blonde hair inside it. Our guy had long blonde hair, and I was very relieved.

After being interviewed by the Detectives, the full story came out now. He had previously worked at the Gasworks Tavern and knew their habits. As the two employees had exited with the night deposit, he robbed them and ran about five blocks south in the laneway, hid his disguise and weapon, and then met us on Carlton Street. I don't know how to explain it and hope Tommy Corbett is out there somewhere to corroborate my story. I don't think I would have believed it if you told it to me.

My Platoon Sergeant was Gord McMechan (aka Gordie Gross). He was a very experienced plainclothes Detective and Investigator. He had supervised the search in the alley and gave me the good news. He just smiled and nodded. Gordie Gross had just made my day and given me his approval.

That night my partner and I caught the Big One.

RAMBO

Sylvester Stallone's movie "Rambo First Blood" was premiering on public television on a summer's Saturday night. My partner for that midnight shift was a young strong Rugby player. Seems like PC Rob Knapper and I were partnered quite often by the Parade Sergeant.

We seemed to click together and, like partners, we anticipated each other's moves. We were dispatched to a little fender bender at Dundas just east of Yonge at Dundas Square. Rob was quickly dealing with this call while I stood on the road covering him from the passing traffic.

I noticed a dark pickup truck turning from Victoria Street onto Dundas without coming to a complete stop at the corner. This was directly in front of me, and I signaled the driver to pull over as I walked to the passenger door of the truck. Rob saw this and quietly moved to just outside the driver's door in his blind spot. No big deal here as I was just going to mention his error and let him continue.

The passenger window was down, and I spoke to the driver saying, "You just failed to stop at the corner." I was looking at the driver and first observed that both of his hands were on the steering wheel and were not a threat to me. He was sitting erect and facing forward but very slowly moved his head to the right to look at me as I spoke to him.

I then noticed his eyes were wide open, and then it looked like something was wrong. Maybe not all his oars were in the water or something else, but he was not on the same channel as me. I quickly scanned the interior of the truck and saw a large paper road map open on the seat and covering the floor area from my view. If his hands stayed on the wheel, there was no threat. His "frozen look" now changed my objective to not cut him loose immediately as planned, and I chose to pursue this fellow further. I now said to him, "Let's have a look at your license for a moment."

Immediately, I saw his right knee raise up about six inches and then slam down onto the gas pedal. The rear tires started to spin, and the forward motion progressed quickly. My mind, get in our car, hit the priority button, announce the pursuit and let's go on a downtown chase. The rugby player had implemented another plan.

He quickly took two long strides and jumped into the back of the pickup while it spun the tires in place and then moved forward. Now Hal is standing there watching his partner leaving in the back of this kid's truck. Thank goodness I had the one, and only, set of scout car keys.

O.K., now I got into my car, activated the siren and roof-lights and announced to the dispatcher, "52(whatever#) …we are east-bound on Dundas Street from Yonge Street in pursuit of a black pickup truck and…MY PARTNER'S IN THE BACK!"

As we approached Church Street, there were about six cars stopped at the east-bound red traffic light. Rob was standing up and holding on to the roof with his left hand, and his right hand was holding his gun to the rear truck window. He was yelling, "Stop! Pull Over!!" The truck then entered the west-bound lanes to pass the stopped traffic and went at full speed through the solid red light. I followed. My brain is thinking, what if he gets through Jarvis Street and then the Don Valley Parkway highway is next? I can't ram the truck, shoot out the tires, and in so many ways, Rob might get ejected upon any impact. Rob can't shoot him through the window without the moving truck going out of control. Very concerning and nothing like I had ever encountered before.

To our surprise, the kid stopped just before Jarvis Street from Rob's demands and my vehicle's presence on his ass. Screw always stopping behind a suspect's vehicle. In this case I passed it and pulled my car in front of the truck blocking it to the curb. I jumped out and Rob planted himself also at the driver's door back on the ground.

We ripped this driver out of that seat and threw him up against the side of his truck. As we searched him, I then had a better look at him and noticed he looked younger than I had first thought and was wearing full green camouflage fatigues. He didn't say a word, and we ejected him into our backseat. A second scout car arrived now for our Assist Call and two Traffic Officers helped us search the truck. I lifted that open road map and saw a stash of survival gear and loaded weapons.

Facing me, when standing on the passenger side earlier, were a loaded double barrel shotgun with the safety off and a carbine .22 calibre rifle loaded with the safety also off. Earlier, if he had taken his hand off the steering wheel, he had only a 12-inch reach to the ready and loaded weapons. Under the guns was a sharpened bundle of sticks as a weapon, knives, tools, wire, pills, snack foods, survival books and many related items.

WTF do we have here? This kid did not talk. He refused to speak and still appeared to be intensely silent and in deep thought. The traffic officers agreed to stay for the tow as we took this warrior to the station.

As we escorted him to the CIB, a passing Officer in the hallway looked at this soldier in his green garb and said, "Who do you think you are?" He replied the only words spoken that night. He said, "RAMBO!"

A registration check, and then a call to his Beaverton home, showed this full-size kid was only 15 years old and had stolen his father's guns and truck.

Earlier that night he had watched the movie First Blood when it debuted on television and then thought he would copy the movie. I guess you don't make sense out of a senseless act, but Sly retreated to the woods in the movie, but this Junior Sly drives from the country to the busiest corner in Canada. Go figure!

The pictures below show the two traffic officers on the left side, Rugby Rob second from the right, and me on the far-right side. The weapons and stash are all laid out on the table. That is Kid Sly in the green war suit.

Of course, he got a slap in Kiddy Court. Rob and I survived, and the Press covered this story. About six months later, we got a Commendation. I think they delayed it because jumping in the back of a fleeing truck is not proper procedure. Go figure!

Our young RAMBO

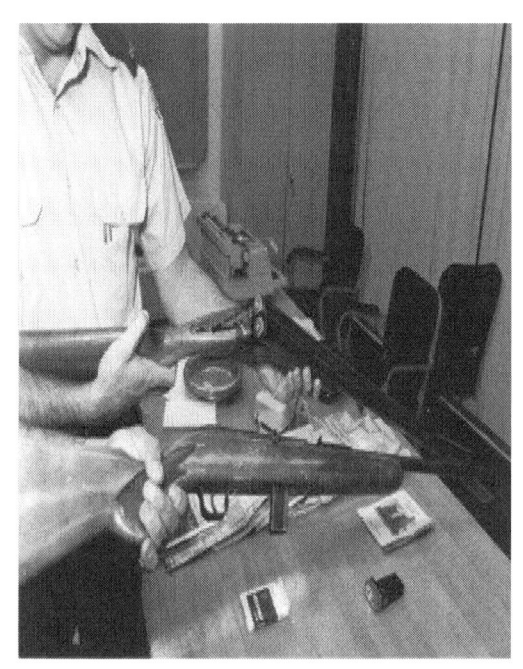

Both fully loaded and safety off.

I am on the far right and Rob Knapper is second from the right.

THE BUS STOP

Pope John Paul II was to hold a Papal Mass at Downsview on October 22, 1984. I had just returned to uniform duties from my years of Intelligence work a few weeks earlier. I was assigned to the midnight shift to guard one set of entrance gates for the next day's Mass. When I arrived, I met an old #52 Division buddy, Hughie Lynn. We had about four other officers working with us at this gate. It was nice to see an old familiar face as I had been "away" for five years. Now this assignment was to ensure the great multitude of people arriving all night long would be orderly. It was a cold and damp night when the gates opened and a few hundred of the faithful entered and were ready to spend the entire night in the fields. They were working on obtaining their best positions for the Mass the next afternoon.

Maybe an hour later, it started to rain, and with the cold temperatures, I'd say about 90 percent of the faithful exited the Park from this very uncomfortable environment. It was my understanding that of the few dozens that stayed, slept under homemade cardboard houses and inside the portable toilets to survive the night. No one was entering the gates now as the weather was so bad. Of the six Police Officers at my gate, we all were huddled under the tent roof canopies erected and manned by the vendors. Hugh and I were not happy campers, and we all started to shake from the cold, wet weather and were going downhill quickly. I still had some attitude from my undercover days and knew there must be a better way.

I remember saying to Hugh, "Come on, let's check this out." We left our post and started to walk into the dark fields for about 20 minutes, and then I saw it!

I'd like to think it had a halo above it, but it was probably just the glow of the light bulb that went off in my head. This "sight" was a full-sized school bus parked in the middle of the large fields as a down centre. The bus had been positioned there for the teenage kids hired by some entrepreneur to sell cigarettes all night to the attendees. Well, there were no customers. The smokers and non-smokers had all bailed out of the park, so the kids used their bus to crash and get some sleep. Hughie and I quietly entered the bus, and I slipped in behind the wheel. I whispered to him, "Shine some light on this stick and we'll see what we've got here."

I knew there were about 6 to 10 kids laid out all over the bus including two making out half-way down the aisle. I then started the bus, and one adolescent teen boy uttered, "Hey, what's happening?" I turned my head to speak to the entire bus and in my loud Police College voice stated, "It's O.K., we're the POLICE!" It worked! There was not another word out of them. I drove that bus slowly over that long bumpy field as Hughie navigated me in the right direction until we found our gate. I signaled for our four buddies to get on the bus, and we filled the first three rows with our kids in the back. Now I think theft is a strong and kind of legal term. I like to use "commandeered" as more appropriate. We were now in Heaven! That protection and that heater made us very comfortable.

We passed on walking to our designated down centre and had the midnight prisoner wagon deliver our box lunches to our bus. For the entire rest of the night, we guarded that gate and watched as no one entered all night long.

Just after sunrise, Mr. Entrepreneur had been searching all over the fields until he came to us, stuck his head inside our bus and asked, "Is this my bus?" I replied, "Yes, and thanks!" We exited the bus and stood by our gate like good soldiers. He drove his kids and our bus away across the fields. All that was left was the white empty lunch boxes remaining on the ground outside of the windows, where they had been dumped by us earlier.

We were relieved by the day shift and went home to sleep as the Pope gave the Mass that afternoon on a Woodstock-style muddy field. I had in my head... "A good Policeman...never goes hungry or cold." We survived, but unfortunately P.C. Hugh Lynn was run down and killed by a driver four years later while on the Don Valley Parkway highway as he was doing a traffic stop.

At least I have those memories of my partner that night.

BLUE LIGHT SPECIAL

I was working a day shift with P.C. Al Downey. We were assigned to a uniform two-man car in the centre of #52 Division when we received a call that a bank had just been robbed at Bay and Queen Street West. We were advised the suspect used a note, no weapon had been seen, and he had just left the bank. No direction of travel had been given.

We were in the area and turned onto Queen Street from Yonge and parked near the cattle crossing (nickname for the busy pedestrian crossover). Al decided to check the area on foot one way, while I went another direction into the Simpsons store. I entered the ground floor of the

Simpsons store and started to eye all the occupants in the Men's Clothing section. One man looked at me with a half glance and then continued to use his hands to check out the hanging suit coats with his back to me. He seemed uninterested that I was there and looking around. I felt my woman's intuition cut in again and walked over towards him. He could fit the very vague description we were given. I shoved him face first into the clothing rack and then grabbed his arm and told him I was going to search him. Well! I remember his face as he fell forward. He looked very surprised and gave me a WTF kind of look. I shoved my hand into his right front pocket and pulled out a large round wad of bills. Maybe a couple of hundred bucks. O.K., maybe possible.

Then out of his left front pocket I pulled out another large wad of bills. Now I could see one, but not two, so I cuffed him and told him he was going to the station with me.

On the way to the car the bank manager ran up to me and said he was, in fact, the guy that had just robbed them. At the station, we examined the evidence further and YES! inside the wad of cash was his hold-up note. We had gone fishing and caught the big one. That's the type of police work I had missed.

EVERYONE WHO...

I met my second bad lawyer. I was living and working in #52 Division and was now well adapted to the diversity of the city. This Brighton/Trenton country boy had been well sensitized to our city and everything diverse in its religion and cultures. Everything had been a first for me to adapt to these new experiences that the city had offered.

As a uniform officer, I was responsible to respond and deal with not only heterosexual domestics but more likely more gay type domestics while policing downtown. I became sensitized to their issues and dealt with each professionally.

On one occasion, two men had been brutally assaulted by three others just for being suspected as gay and walking along on a street downtown one night. I caught the three and charged them accordingly. Two were heading to Juvenile court while the third was in adult court. There were no Detectives in court that day, so I was the Officer in Charge for this Gay Bashing case.

The victim was a pleasant young man and a true victim of these thugs. I had seen the lawyer representing the adult accused around the court before and he had never impressed me. This man stood tall and puffed out his chest and let it be known he was some sort of a Judo expert. He decided to try and go after me on the stand when I submitted his client's statement, which was very incriminating. In his cross examination, he started right away by saying, "Officer, this occurred in the Church and Wellesley area, and as everyone knows, it's known as Vaseline Alley." I advised I had never heard that term used for that area. He said, "Well, everyone knows that area is Vaseline Alley." I replied that I had worked in that area for many years and had never heard that phrase ever being used. I started to feel that this lawyer might be like his client and was starting to show homophobic tendencies. Was it just me or am I in redneck territory? He finally moved on with his questioning, but it got worse. He now asked me, "Officer, isn't it true that everyone that lives in Church and Wellesley is gay?" I replied I didn't think this was the case. He asked again, and again I gave the same answer. I had enough of this Bozo and decided to professionally shut him down.

It was the third time that he asked the same question, "Now Officer, you have worked in this area for many years, and isn't it true that everyone that lives in the Church and Wellesley area is gay?"

I turned away from him and looked directly at the Judge and stated calmly, "Your Honor, I can advise that I live at Church and Wellesley, Sir, and can tell the Court that I am not gay!" The Court Reporter was gagging into her recorder strapped to her face, the citizens in the court started to laugh, and the Judge also laughed and then stopped himself. The lawyer froze and tried to comprehend what had just happened. It took him a few minutes because he was thick.

I gave up some of my personal security that day, but it was for a greater cause. I did not have to go into details, but I lived in a high-rise apartment on Dundonald Street. This was one block above and overlooking the corner of Church and Wellesley Streets. On Gay Pride weekends, I would have to stay in my apartment. This was so my fellow officers would not see me heading to the beer store or cleaners and think I was attending the event. That was just not done in those days.

The Judge finally said, "Counselor, you have asked, and he has answered your question. I think it is in your best interest to move on." The lawyer was pissed, and you could almost see the well-deserved ostrich egg dripping down his chin. Normally I don't keep score, but I won the case that day and felt good for the young man that had been victimized by his client. I would think he was a Legal Aid lawyer, and he never earned my respect.

FATHER KNOWS WORST

This guy didn't deserve a Father's Day present. I was working in the #52 Division Criminal Investigative Bureau (C.I.B.) and my partner was Detective Leo Henry. He was a seasoned veteran, an old-school Englishman, my former Patrol Sergeant, and a great guy. We worked together for a year and a half while I was training with him and later waiting on the Promotional list. Frequently, on the midnight shift, we would get a call to attend a smaller Division that didn't have a C.I.B. working 24/7. This night, we would get a call to investigate a Police Shooting in #51 Division.

Buddy drives onto Jarvis Street and engages in a conversation with a young hooker. She enters his car and they drive off. Unknown to him, two Old Clothes Constables watched this transaction and followed them. The car quietly pulls into a small parking lot in the centre of St. Jamestown in the Sherbourne and Wellesley area. The car parks in a space and the Officers watch. They waited and decided now would be a good time to quietly approach the vehicle. As they got closer, they could hear the female as she had just started to scream for help. Something bad was happening inside this car, and they started to run towards it with their firearms drawn. As the car started to move forward, she jumped out at about the same time he was driving it directly at the Officers.

They had shouted, "Stop Police!" and then felt they were forced to fire several shots at the car as he was now using it as a weapon against them. The hooker had rolled out, and the car sped off as the Officers were diving to avoid being hit by it.

Leo and I were detailed to handle the entire investigation including the Firearm Discharge Report. We attended the scene and interviewed the hooker. She felt that the Officers saved her life as she had been terrified by the man inside the car. The vehicle description was broadcast city-wide and the Officers were providing us with their details of the incident. The firearms were seized, and we headed back to our C.I.B. to work on it further. A few hours later, we were advised our car had been located. It was parked on Gerrard Street, just east of University between the hospitals. We now wondered if he had been shot.

After a vehicle registration, we checked the area and found him. This is where it gets weird. This "father" had a seriously injured child at their northern Ontario city. The child and its mother were flown down south by Air Ambulance to Sick Kids Hospital. Dad had to load his second child, a young boy, into their car and make the long drive south. He was to re-join his wife and find out the condition of his sick child. When he entered the big city, Dad goes directly to Jarvis Street and, while his son is sleeping in the back of the car, makes a deal with a hooker. They get into a fight in the car, she screams and then jumps out of the moving car. Dad speeds off at the Old Clothes Officers dodging bullets. Remember his son is in the back of this car sleeping with bullets being shot at it.

A few bullet holes in the car and a flat tire later, he limps his vehicle to the hospital and meets his wife. He was brought to our office and charged appropriately. This man did not get or deserve any respect from us. We ensured he had to return to Toronto once more, for Court!

THE BEST/WORST DAY

The best day of my life was also the worst day of my life. I was fortunate to have been attached to 52 C.I.B. and working for a year and a half with Detective Leo Henry. The Promotional Competition to Sergeant had been announced, and I threw my hat into the ring. After our Unit submitted their recommendations, I was granted a Promotional Interview. The three-man Board of Senior Officers had been sitting for two-and-a-half weeks of interviews, and I was scheduled as the last interview on the last day. I could only assume they would be tired of listening to the same answers to the same questions for 12 long days. Not good for me. I studied hard, polished the boots and leather and prepared myself. The day finally came. I walked into this little room and first thought there was no way they could see my boots from behind their desk and what a waste of time that was.

I had envisioned the three to be like Lt. Colonel Henry Blake on MASH with their lure-filled fishing hats on and a pole in one hand and looking forward to this being the end of the Board and the weekend off.

The first Senior Officer welcomed me and stated the known, "Do you realize you are the last Officer to be appearing in front of this Board?" I replied, "Yes, Sir." He then said, "I guess we can say we have saved the best for the last!" I quickly replied, "Sir, you have seen the rest, now you are seeing the best!" I later thanked the man upstairs that they laughed! Then we got down to business. I tried to give them answers that they had not heard and was successful. I had made the pending Promotional list to Sergeant and now waited for the official nod to come months later. The main thing was to stay out of trouble during that time.

Some 12 years earlier, my Father and Mother had been at my Aylmer graduation and were always proud of their Toronto Policeman son. This accomplishment made my Father especially proud as he had retired as a Sergeant with the Royal Canadian Air Force (R.C.A.F.) He knew I had made the list, and we both waited the required months.

That was June, and in January of the next year, I was still waiting patiently. The Unit Commander had returned me to #52 Division uniform patrol duties, so I had to be cautious on the street. No Complaints! Be Good!

In January, my Father became ill and I used all my time bank to stay in Trenton for three weeks and drove to Kingston Hospital ICU daily with my Mother. He had pancreatitis and was going downhill. I had to return to work, and my Inspector asked me for an update. When I told him, he said, "You don't belong here. Go home and I will book you off sick for as long as you need it." Thank you, Sir!

Another week in Trenton and me, being the only son, had to make the decision to let nature take its course and stop the suffering. I was just about to leave for the hospital the next morning when the phone rang at our house in Trenton. I made sure I answered it and was advised he had passed on. I then told my Mother and sisters in the next room. This was the day after his 65th birthday. I called my Police Station and advised I would be off now on Bereavement Leave.

Not 30 minutes later, my Inspector called me to advise me my Promotion to the rank of Sergeant had just come through. I was advised to report on the midnight shift at #51 Division (Regent Park) a few days later. It was a hard day of emotions, and my oldest sister walked into the room with my Father's RCAF Sergeant chevrons and gave them to me. We took care of business during the few next days, and I returned to Toronto.

I showed up at #51 Division, wearing a suit, for the midnight shift, and Sergeant Tony Brannon showed me around the Division. The next night, I had obtained a new Sergeant's uniform and was solo on 51S1.

During the next few months, I tried to avoid calls to hospitals and thought how the older street people, eating out of garbage bins, were immune to every disease known to man.

I had received a letter of congratulations from the Chair of the Toronto Police Services Board, and he also noted at the same time his condolences. Word travels fast and far in our environment, and my situation was unique and somewhat well known by now. All that mattered to me was that "He knew!"

My father, Roy Cunningham with me at my 1975 Graduation in Aylmer, Ontario.

CHAPTER FOUR

AS A SERGEANT AND STAFF SERGEANT
(1987-2003)
No. 51 Division (Sergeant -1987)
No. 13 Division (Staff Sergeant -1992)
No. 53 Division (Staff Sergeant -2000)

HUMOUR IN UNIFORM

I paraded my #51 Division officers for the midnight shift. One of my guys had a See and Say (Barnyard Edition) and kept pulling the cord during our Parade. I asked him to put it away, so we could conclude our briefing. About four hours later, at about 3 a.m., I was doing a solo stealth patrol through the centre walkways of Regent Park. It was then that I heard the Pig, the Rooster, and the Cow. These sounds were echoing off the three-story residences of Regent Park using the police car's Public-Address System. I decided it was time for Sgt51 to leave and check the parking lots at Cherry Beach. You've got to love good Police humour.

Sometimes a prank was not required but something they did to themselves. The nicest "newfie" recruit had some time on the job and worked at a western Division. She was detailed to deliver a package to the downtown Police Headquarters on College Street.

She was somewhat geographically challenged and stopped her marked police car on a downtown street to ask a citizen how to get to Police Headquarters. She was a sweetie and made the mistake of telling at least one other copper back at the station what had occurred.

Years earlier, I recall my first solo DOA (Dead on Arrival-Sudden Death) that had me reassuring the landlady I could handle her tenant's hot summer decaying body. As we got higher up each step of her stairs, I gagged more and more with the dry heaves. It was so embarrassing when I had to stick my rookie head out of the hallway window.

Us lucky Supervisors had to go to all the DOA calls. One of them in a #51 Division high rise was so bad. You entered the floor for the apartment and you smelt it immediately. On the ride down, a lady entered the elevator on a much lower floor, and you could tell I stunk and she was not impressed. That was a great way to start the 10-hour shift, walking around smelling like a bad dead body.

Sergeant, #51 Division 1987-1992

GOING POSTAL

In 1987 I had been recently promoted to Sergeant and had been detailed to a special assignment in 55 Division. Canada Post was in a strike position and lock-out with C.U.P.W., their Postal Union. A special dedicated unit was detailed to handle the picket lines. The Officer in Charge was Staff Sgt. J. Fantino, and Sgt. James Knowlton and I were the two Supervisors along with a couple of dozen Officers. Jim Knowlton had some previous strike training and experience and taught us all some quick formations and tactics. This was years ahead of the Public Order Unit being formed.

The entrance on Eastern Avenue was totally blocked by a small group of picketers at all times of the day and night. If they anticipated any movement, they had the methods of getting a large group there within maybe 30 minutes. The concern was scabs being allowed into the plant during the strike to do their work. I heard talk of perhaps using helicopters to get workers into the plant. As it was, the line was difficult. Each time a management employee or truck would approach the line, the strikers would totally block the entrance. Fantino worked out an agreement where they had, I think it was ten minutes per vehicle, to stop the car and then allow it to enter. I recall during this time, the officers and myself were subjected to the worst insults and language out of the mouths of men and women. We were called every name you could imagine but were professional enough to totally ignore it all.

One "lady" made sure to ask us if we were taking our heroin and shooting up all the time. This was a topical issue related to a recent event where two undercover Toronto Police Officers were found in their car with needles in their arms. I recall asking one officer to leave the line and take a break. I could see that they were getting to him, and we didn't need an explosion of anger to set things off.

The line was quiet one minute and then, when something occurred, it grew quickly and became very tense at times. In these days, the Police facilitated Management by allowing entry onto the sites, meaning each entry was a confrontational encounter with the strikers. We kept hearing the rumours that a large group of illegal workers (scabs) were being gathered to bring into the plant.

One afternoon, about three school buses arrived on Eastern Avenue. These were old tired, used school buses from Quebec. These "buses" were full of illegal workers that Management had hired to work in the plant. I learned later that someone had bought these old used buses and equipped them for this transport detail. We opened the line at the gate to allow them entry and the strikers threw eggs, wood and anything within their reach at these buses. Some of the officers were hit with the eggs. I made sure I patted down the strikers with eggs in their pockets just to see them squirm. After a lot of cursing and yelling, the buses entered the compound, and the line was very upset for some time. The next eight to ten hours were tense and the line swelled to maybe 50 to 80 protesters. They wanted a piece of these scabs when they left. We expected an ugly exit sometime that evening.

Unknown to us, some fine Toronto Police Traffic Officer had located these buses and removed their licence plates as unsafe vehicles. I don't know if he did that on his own initiative or it came from higher up, but life was about to get very difficult for us. We didn't know how these scabs were going to exit the building that night, and I don't think anyone had a plan. I'd be fine with them staying there for the next month or as long as the strike took to end.

It was around 11 p.m. when we heard they were coming out. Apparently, there was one bus available, but passengers were not allowed on it as it was not legal. Jim Knowlton came up with a plan.

It was so ridiculous that it just might work. Just inside the gate, the one bus was parked ready to exit and two lines of Police Officers formed, one on each back corner of the bus. We had maybe twenty Officers, so that was two lines of ten on each side. We had all the scabs standing inside these two lines and started walking for the gate. The Officers manning the striker's entrance opened the line of picketers just enough to "squeeze" the bus, the police and the scabs walking through the opening to Eastern Avenue. They were waiting in force for us but didn't really know how to handle this. They yelled and screamed and tried to throw a few projectiles, but it stayed mostly verbal. We made it through the line onto Eastern Avenue, but now what do we do? I just remembered us at close quarters in a quick march with these pale white-faced scabs. There was not much between us and them being severely beaten by a large group of angry people that hated them.

I don't know if we used Knox Avenue or how we got there, but we arrived at Queen and Greenwood Avenue. We didn't know what to do now, but we understood a group of 50 to 100 yelling strikers had walked along with us the whole way to Queen Street. They were looking for a break or weak point in our formation to attack. As we walked east on Queen Street after 11 p.m. that night, we saw it! There it was! A TTC (Toronto Transit Commission) bus at the corner about to go north on Greenwood. One of the officers ran to it and had the driver stop and wait. This was the start of his route, so it was empty. We commandeered this bus in the name of Her Majesty Queen Elizabeth.

The scabs were quickly ejected onto the bus, and the driver looked dazed, as his bus was now filled and not one paid or showed a Metro Pass. He was ordered to drive directly to the Danforth subway station without stopping. We figured he could bill Canada Post after the trip. He was told to take off and drive away quickly. The protesters and the police were without vehicles, so no one could follow the TTC bus as it sped away northbound on Greenwood Avenue. Talk about timing and good luck. This was not the ending that I had expected, and it ended up well for all concerned. That was the last time they tried to bring in scabs, and the strike did end about a week later. Jim's plan worked and then we "improvised".

Future strikes manned by Toronto Police took the approach that if Management wants to force vehicles and people being allowed to enter their sites, they would have to get evidence.

They then would have to go to the Courts and get a Judge's Court Order that we would then enforce.

We would no longer intervene between the two sides or take one side over the other.

We had a great team and survived under some very difficult circumstances.

AT THE SUMMIT

My new duties as a Uniform Supervisor would be interrupted for six months as I was selected for another special detail. My Unit Commander chose me to work with the R.C.M.P. as a Security Planner for the upcoming 14th G7 Summit to be held in Toronto between June 19 and 21, 1988. The venue for the Summit was the Metro Convention Centre.

I attended security briefings with the R.C.M.P. starting in the winter months of 1987-1988. The Convention Centre, and each of the seven hotels hosting a Delegation, required a Security Planning Team consisting of one R.C.M.P. and one Toronto Police Sergeant. I was assigned the Royal Canadian Yacht Club (R.C.Y.C.) on Centre Island where the dinner was to be held and the "group photo" was to be taken showing the Toronto skyline in the background. An R.C.M.P. Sergeant was assigned as my planning partner.

I called the Toronto Marine Unit to provide me several cold boat rides across the Toronto Harbour to the icy R.C.Y.C. dock in January. This was only possible on the days that the ice floe left an open space in the harbour.

My R.C.M.P. partner seemed to be always MIA (Missing in Action) when I went over there to work. I was recording the utility mains, escape routes, fire systems, posting positions for the manpower, and all other related security requirements. As the work progressed over the next few months, it became apparent that the Prime Minister's Office (P.M.O.) would have to be advised that this site would have to be cancelled.

The Toronto Inner Harbour would have to be swept, secured and closed at least 48 hours prior to the Delegates taking the ferry ride to the yacht club. Two of the main island ferries would have to be shut down during that time. The small bridge to the yacht club was not big enough to allow access for the President of the United States' armoured limo. Use of a helicopter had been ruled out as the only landing zone nearby was gravel and too close to the yachts. The limo and helicopter were essential as there was no Safe House near the yacht club. Finally, the members would not allow the police dogs to search their boats for explosives prior to the event. My two months of hard work had been a learning experience. Fact is, as bad as the P.M.O.'s office wanted that balcony picture, the Secret Service would never allow Reagan to go there. The site was cancelled, and the dinner was now to be held at the University of Toronto and the group picture would be taken there.

I worked for Superintendent Dave Cowan and Staff Sergeant Jim Bamford. They identified the need to deal with the anticipated demonstrations outside of each venue. My new assignment was to work with my new TPS partner Fitz and plan the response to demonstrators anywhere at any time during the Summit.

The R.C.M.P. would not be involved in this task. Toronto Police commenced training hundreds of officers in the first class of our new Public Order

Unit. This had not been done before, and we needed a full compliment of trained and equipped Riot trained officers. Staff Superintendent Bob Molyneaux was the man chosen to start this program and lead them during the Summit.

Since most of those officers would be under my Response Plan during the Summit, I attended the first class and received the full training also. I have one note regarding the training. Although the training in Crowd Dynamics, Crowd Control and De-Escalation techniques were valuable, one Instructor crossed the line. While lecturing us, he advised that Emergency Task Force snipers would be positioned on rooftops, and if someone was about to throw a Molotov Cocktail at us, he advised, "The sniper would take him out!" I looked around and some of the younger officers were buying this. Sell us a new program, but don't B.S. a B.S'er. This would never occur, and let's keep it real here. I enjoyed my P.O.U. (Public Order Unit) training and performed with them as a Supervisor for many years after receiving the course.

Fitz and I developed our Response Plan. We addressed the first ever Mass Arrest Program and Mass Prisoner Processing, identified our staff as 250 P.O.U. trained officers and 200 regular uniform Officers. We acquired a large fully equipped Down Centre for our personnel on the University of Toronto property. Furthermore, we obtained prisoner buses and Court Security/Prisoner transport officers and many other required details. The company gave us rooms at a very nice downtown hotel during the Summit.

The Summit was progressing well with Reagan, Mulroney, Thatcher and the others enjoying their meetings and dinners downtown. The big day came on the weekend for the demonstrators.

Fitz and I were in our Mobile Command Centre parked at Queen and University. We had a Radio Room dispatcher helping with the dialogue between our Supervisors, P.O.U., Regular Officers and the Plainclothes Crowd Infiltration Unit.

Intelligence was obtained and passed on that the demonstrators were to march from Queens Park, down University Avenue towards the Convention Centre. Supt. Molyneaux and his men were ready. They drew a line at south-bound University Avenue and Dundas Street, and they would be stopped there. Fitz and I had a front row seat from our Command Post and then detailed our Prisoner buses to back up to the barriers erected on University Avenue.

The momentum was growing, and the timing couldn't be worse. My partner Fitz and I had joked about this for months prior to this day. His wife was pregnant, and they were expecting their first child, and sure enough, at that exact moment, he got the call and had to leave. I never asked, but I hope he named the child "Summit."

Our P.O.U. did its first ever response and arrested about 300 demonstrators that day at those barriers without any incidents. The front-page coverage by the Toronto newspapers the next day showed a majestic Superintendent Robert Molyneaux leading his P.O.U. troops forward with his bullhorn in hand.

Everything went as Fitz and I had hoped and planned. Supt. Dave Cowan gave us both a 40-hour award for our six months of work on this project. Jim Bamford offered me a permanent position as a District Planner. I respectfully declined, as I was a street cop and missed being on the road with my men.

REACHING THE HEIGHTS

Attempted Suicide calls were commonplace. One of my first was as a young Constable in 52 Division. There was a high-rise apartment building on Dundonald Street. A few years earlier, a sniper, on top of the same building, was firing down at me and others one day. This time when I returned, it was a lady threatening to jump off her balcony. Of the 20-plus stories, I figured she was maybe on about the 15 floor. Three of us approached her door. By opening the mail slot, we could see her pacing back and forth towards an open balcony door. She refused to open her door for us. I used the apartment next door to gain access to the double balcony. As I climbed onto the outside balcony railing, Constable Rick Tulloch was behind me and grabbed the back of my gun-belt. This threw me off somewhat, but he let go as I reached her balcony. By standing outside on top of the railing itself, I could manoeuvre around the steel partition onto her balcony. I made sure I didn't look down at any time.

There was no time to think, just react. I ran down her hallway inside her apartment and grabbed her. I guess Rick had time to think and look down. I had not expected him to follow me, and he had not. Later, while outside, Rick approached me and said, "Hal, I'll go down any dark laneway with you and back you up anytime. I just couldn't do what you just did." I hadn't given it a second thought and knew he always had my back and more common sense than I did.

Years later I was a Supervisor in #51 Division and all my cars were tied up as there were pending priority calls. I advised the dispatcher I would take the call to the men's downtown hostel at the Seaton House.

They had a client threatening to jump out of an upper floor window. I walked down the hall, and there were about five staff members and one Ambulance attendant talking to a man. He was sitting on the window ledge with half of his body outside and the other half still inside. They all looked my way and gave me that "Oh, good. The Police are here!" look. I approached the open window and started a conversation with the man. He was outside, but his top half was behind the open window to me. I looked at the Ambulance attendant and winked so the man could not see it.

I quickly lurched forward and grabbed the man, and the Ambulance attendant quickly followed and grabbed him also. I banged the man's head against the window before we dragged him back inside to the floor. Everyone was happy, and I left. I almost wanted to rub my two hands together and go, "There!"

It took about 65 seconds to resolve this situation to a positive outcome. I went on to the next pending call.

One other evening in #51 Division, I was patrolling in an unmarked Warrant car as the Road Supervisor. I liked this stealth mode around Regent Park as it gave me the advantage to see more. It was after dark during the early evening when I pulled onto Dundas Street from River Street towards the Don Valley Parkway highway. As I was driving across the bridge over the DVP, I saw a man standing on the outside of the concrete railing. He was facing away from the bridge with his hands behind his back holding the railing.

I parked on the far east end of the bridge and turned my lights off. I radioed for another car to meet me on the bridge with a silent approach. I removed my spring jacket and gun belt and left them in the car. I was wearing a dark blue sweater without shoulder flashes or markings and had dark pants on. I was now in the stealth mode with no police markings. He would have to have better lighting to see I was a police officer.

I approached this man and started an innocent conversation, I believe about the weather. He was not into having any conversation and just let me talk. He kept looking down towards the highway and river. We always said if the cars don't kill you, the Don River water will! I could see to the west end of the bridge as a marked police scout car pulled up quietly with their lights off, and two officers were approaching us slowly.

I could only see the first officer, Tim Houchen, as the other smaller officer was eclipsed by Big Tim. He was one of several guys from British Columbia we hired, and I'd swear he was built like a lumberjack.

I had the jumper's attention as he was looking east, my way, and Tim was approaching from the west. So, at the exact right moment, I said to the jumper, "Have you met my friend Tim?" He then looked to the west at Sasquatch who was walking into his view. I then grabbed over the railing and wrapped my arms around the jumper. His response was to let go of the railing and then all his weight dropped to just my grasp around his body.

I had to lock my two knees into the vertical slots in the concrete railing posts to maintain our balance between my knees and my arms. I could stop his intended fall, but not for long. Tim reacted to us now by rushing the distance forward to meet our two bodies. The big bear wrapped his two huge arms around both the jumper and myself, hoisted us up in the air over the railing and then slam-dunked us onto the sidewalk. I was at the bottom of all the weight of Tim and the jumper. The sidewalk I landed on had a six-inch drop to the roadway. That transition of six inches from the sidewalk to roadway was centred in the middle of my back.

The two officers secured the man and took him to the puzzle factory for a realignment of the satellite dish. Me? Three days off with a back injury. Tim did the right thing, and I was proud of his actions.

We give this job our best years, but with incidents like this, several rough bar fights, too many hours in a police car, two car accidents, etc, all on the job, we do feel it in our advanced years.

In the end, we deserve that pension as we proudly do our jobs.

RIDE-ALONGS

Ride-Alongs were an opportunity to let others see our city though our eyes. I became a fan of taking interested parties out on ride-alongs in my police vehicle over my last 15 years. We love our job, and anyone else that wants to acquire first-hand knowledge must do one of these. I have had everything from dispatchers, reporters, students, friends and family on these ventures.

The dispatchers loved getting out and seeing our side of it and feeling the rush during a good call. I enjoyed every one of them in my car in #51 and #13 Divisions. During one of them, there was a Beer Store strike, and Regent Park was getting very tense. We were on patrol and attended the Beer Store on Gerrard Street for an alarm. I ensured she, the dispatcher, was safely positioned in the car but still with a view of the store. I grabbed my shotgun and entered the Beer Store and apprehended two guys doing the B & E (Break and Enter) for a few cases of beer. Arriving now as my backup were members of a patrolling ETF3 (Emergency Task Force- Gun Truck).

I guess these citizens never realized you could go to any L.C.B.O. (Liquor Control Board of Ontario) and buy six-packs of American beer during these strikes. We did for our choir practices after work on the waterfront.

My neighbour Gill was an older retired Air Canada executive and expressed an interest in a night out with me. He joined me in #51 Division, and it was one crazy summer's night. We attended a crack house, disturbances, fights, and one call after another. At the end of the night, he stated, "You know, I drive through this area almost every day and never knew until now what it is really like." Gill had been educated to our world and left with a very positive impression of how we do our job. I lost him to a brain tumour the next year but was so pleased we had our night together. I had shared my world with him through my eyes that night.

Some of you may recall the #14 Division Supervisor that offered to take one of our Police Commissioners out on the road for the experience. Even though I'm sure he, and all of us, had little respect for that Commissioner, he wanted to show the Comm. what it was like. The offer was never accepted, and the Comm. continued to direct future policy decisions based on no real experience of our job.

I always thought that any officer on the job that wanted to show their married partner what he/she endures daily, then they should consider an evening on the road together. Yes, it might not be the right choice for some, but if they both choose to be together, it should happen.

I offered this to my platoon officers, but no one ever carried through with it. Maybe a structured volunteer program would remove any stigma that might be attached.

THE CORONER'S OFFICE

There was a strange initiation to those new members of the Forensic Identification Unit. The new officer would be advised he was required to attend the Coroner's Office and fingerprint a recently deceased hooker. Upon arrival at the Coroner's Office, he would be led to the steel vaults and the appropriate drawer would be opened. It would reveal a large black zippered body-bag. The officer would slowly start to unzip the bag when the body inside would jump up and scream. The officer usually screamed, jumped back a step and assumed the fighter stance. Everyone was on the floor laughing. The plan was to place a clerk from the Coroner's Office inside the bag and then close him inside the steel cabinets with all the other dead bodies. He would have only ten minutes of available air in the bag. This was all caught on a video camera stationed down the hallway from the drawers.

I personally saw one of those videos with two very frightened victims caught on camera. Those videos have been cautiously held from others getting a prized copy.

P.S. There are no inside walls dividing the compartments with full exposure of all the other dead bodies. Sick puppies!

THE VIADUCT

As a young Sergeant, I was required to attend all Sudden Death occurrences. We had a variety of "jumper" calls while working near and under the Bloor Street Viaduct. My partner attended two different ones. Early morning commuters on the subway train could see a body below in the bushes. When Sgt. B. arrived on scene down below, to his surprise, the dead body spoke. In a very low voice, the man that had been lying there all night whispered to Sgt. B. "Am I still alive?" He was transported to the hospital and was one of only a few to survive the plunge.

Months later, there was a case of a wheelchair found on top of the bridge. An inspection below revealed the deceased body. It appeared that he had used his wheelchair to roll to the top of the bridge and then jumped over the side. The investigation revealed that he had been a survivor of an earlier jump and returned the second time. There will not be a third! I'm not sure, but I always wondered if this was Sgt. B.'s bush survivor that had returned.

On one midnight shift, Doug Corrigan, our civilian police tow truck driver was driving across the bridge at about 2 a.m. He saw the Cadillac parked on the bridge, and it was locked and unoccupied. His suspicions were proven correct when he used his spotlight to locate the deceased below the bridge laying in a stone culvert.

I met Doug at the top and then had one of my cars locate the body at the bottom. Our records showed a recent missing person report had been submitted by a Willowdale family regarding their missing father/husband. He had been very ill with cancer. It appears he snuck out in the middle of the night and ended the pain for himself. I was on route to notify the family when a #54 Division car radioed me to say they had been stopped by the adult son looking for his Dad. I told them to advise the son the Dad had been located and was now back home. I entered the house and met a very strong Italian wife and her adult daughter. I told them of their loved one's fate and what was to happen next.

Just as I finished, the son had just arrived home and I now had to advise him. I apologized for misleading him but was concerned that he could drive home first, and then I would let him know when he was safely back home. I felt very sorry for the family, and they knew the pain their husband/father had suffered, and he now was at peace.

It was over one month later that I received a call to attend a funeral parlor just up north of us in #53 Division. When I arrived, the funeral director led me to his office where the Italian widow lady from last month was waiting. She had a request of me and wanted it to go through the funeral home first.

She wanted me to take her below the Bloor Viaduct to the exact location of her husband's death. I had dealt with some personal family death issues recently and understood her request, and it was not an unusual one that people make.

Some will travel halfway around the world to see the exact place of death.

I tried to convince her to have her daughter or son attend with us for family support, but she refused. It was to be just her and me to attend. I drove her in my marked Supervisor's car to Bayview Avenue below the bridge. There were some workers in the area looking at us and wondering what we were doing. I parked in a nice grassy area and said that it was the location. She immediately corrected me by saying her husband had been marked by landing on stones and the culvert in front of us must have been the spot. I had been outmaneuvered and admitted she must be correct. We silently held hands in the front of that police car while she cried softly.

With her required knowledge, she told me to drive her back to her car at the funeral home as she has "things to do." I couldn't talk her into letting me drive her back home to Willowdale. She wouldn't have it as she was too busy and had things to do, places to go. She was so strong, and I admired her. There is no training for how to handle these situations.

THE HARDEST THING

This was one of the hardest things I had to do. The interesting thing about #51 Division was its diversity. The south was waterfront and docks, the center was the Regent Park Housing Project, rooming houses mixed in with the Cabbagetown townhouses, and the high-density housing in St. Jamestown. Finally, above Bloor Street were the very affluent homes of Rosedale. It made policing in these areas interesting as you had to adapt to your clients as you drove north. It was just different people with different problems.

My Staff Sergeant chose his young Sergeant for the detail he had just received on his desk. I had the information in the message and headed north. It was mid-evening in the winter time, and I located a very nice large Rosedale mansion that had the right street number on it. I took a moment and then knocked on the door. I could see lights coming on and the door opened. A middle-aged couple answered the door, and I asked if I could enter and speak to them.

After verifying their identity and that of their son, I got directly to the point. I advised them I had a message from the O.P.P. (Ontario Provincial Police) that it was suspected that their adult son and his adult male friend had drowned under the ice in a northern Ontario lake. They had been making a winter scuba ice dive and failed to return to the hole and were still under the lake's ice covering.

It was expected that a police helicopter would assist with the search the next day to locate and recover the two bodies. We sat in silence for some time. I felt so sad for their loss and gave them lots of time.

I then called the O.P.P. up north for them and established contact. They got on the phone and had a few questions to ask them directly as to what was to occur the next morning. The parents thanked me for helping them with the contact and advising them of the news.

I left with a very heavy heart but knew I had to allow my coping skills to kick in and return to my duties.

It was over one month later that I received a letter at the station. It was a Thank You card from the husband and wife. The message stated how difficult it must have been on me, and they wished me all the best and thanked me again for assisting them during their difficult time.

Imagine that, thinking of and thanking me, with everything in their lives that had changed. I held that card for many years in a special place in my heart. Words spoken are one thing but as the York Regional Police motto states, "DEEDS SPEAK." To say I was humbled would be an understatement. I quite often think of those two people to this day, some 30 years later.

CHERRY BEACH

My favourite shift to work was the midnight shift. As a Uniform Supervisor on patrol in the Housing Project areas, good police work opportunities were available after the bars closed and the streets were quiet. I could quickly respond to radio calls, and it seemed that it was mostly just police officers, hookers, drug dealers and other criminals that were not in bed at that time.

I made certain that, at least once during my shift, I would cruise to the south end of the Division and make sure all was good at Cherry Beach. Over the years, I found that you could expect the unexpected at Cherry Beach. There were beach parties in the summer and some of them were "our boys" having a good time.

There would always be parked cars in the parking lot corners. I found every combination of man/woman, man/man, woman/woman couples all saying they were just talking, even though their clothes were on the floor of their cars. I felt it was my responsibility to ensure the women were of age and there of their own free will. If you don't want the bright spotlights of a police car to surprise you, then get a room!

A young group was drinking on the beach one summer's night, and I drove my car onto the sand to ask them to move the party elsewhere. A few minutes later, they were nice enough to push my big white car out of the deep sand and back onto the parking lot. It saved me the embarrassment of calling a tow truck over the police radio. They were good kids and we all were young once. I told them to party on.

It was another nice hot summer's night at about 4 a.m. I quietly pulled into the first parking lot of Cherry Beach. It seemed that all the late-night cars were now gone and there was no one left in the park. I drove to the east end of the lot, and that's when I saw it!

I readily noticed a very large fire truck in the centre of the parking lot. It was one of those hoist type trucks that lifts a large basket maybe 80 feet in the air. The four long legs to stabilize it were fully extended on each side of the unit. Did I mention that every red light on this thing was flashing in all four directions illuminating the entire area of this parking lot? Since there was no smoke, I knew there was not a fire, and this unit looked totally abandoned. What the hell was I walking into?

I exited my car cautiously and approached the big shiny red truck. I saw that it had a decal on the door of some other fire department, not Toronto Fire. Was it stolen? It was very quiet, and no one was here but me and my new truck.

A very quiet female giggle was heard above me, and then a male voice saying, "Shhh!" This investigator immediately knew it was coming from this raised bucket up in the trees. Now I'm not the smartest man, but I now recall hearing about a Fire Convention in town. O.K., some lady was getting her ultimate fantasy filled at 80 feet, lights and all! I guess this is the fireman's calendar version of the Mile-High club.

I retreated to my car and was now heading back to the housing projects to check on my drug dealers and hookers. During the next few days, I was relieved to not hear of the theft of a big red fire truck. Ya, I guess they were just talking, too.

THE ROPE WAS TOO LONG

A Bloor Street viaduct jumper learned a valuable lesson. It was a summertime weekday afternoon in #51 Division when I received a call of a jumper on the Bloor Street viaduct. Upon arrival, I could see a bright yellow nylon rope tied around the stone railing and hanging over the side. The rope was approximately 30 feet long and just contained a noose on the far end. No body hanging? I drove to the bottom and parked on the bicycle path. According to witnesses that had been driving along Bayview Avenue, they "saw something big fall and then something small." The Ambulance had now arrived, and they had only one sheet to cover the body from public view. I chose the part with the "Oh Shit! deer in the headlight" look to cover the head with the sheet. I carried it like a basketball wrapped in a towel to the waiting ambulance. One should take note that if you are going to hang yourself from great heights, don't use a long rope. The weight of your body falling from 30 feet will snap like a bullwhip at the Calgary Stampede when you reach that exact distance. It will decapitate your head in a nice clean cut and leave the noose empty of any package. Just saying.

DANGEROUS GUN CALLS

Myself and my officers made the six o'clock news. I tried to ensure that I passed on a lot of my firearms, tactical and surveillance training skills that I had learned. I made sure our officers were "tuned up" to work as a team on dangerous Gun Calls. They did perform as a team and only used safe practices to do each gun call "by the numbers." Rarely did we request the assistance of the ETF

(Emergency Task Force) unless shots had been fired or it turned into a barricaded situation.

On one day shift in #51 Division, it was reported a man in the restaurant at the corner of Parliament and Dundas Street had a gun concealed under his jacket. We responded to the area and the first car parked across the street in the gas station lot advised us of his observations on the front door.

The other cars quickly filled in to the four compass points, each one block away and out of view. I was unable to obtain a plainclothes unit to attend the call and enter the restaurant. It was left up to our marked cars and uniform officers to handle this call. At least no one was rushing in foolishly. All trained practices of communication, concealment and cover were being utilized. Suddenly, our car watching the front announced that our suspect had exited the restaurant and was entering a taxi cab. The suspect boarded the cab, and they were now driving east-bound on Dundas Street from Parliament.

No one noticed that about four marked police cars quickly fell into position behind the cab. As he was stopping for a red light at River Street, I advised we would do a high risk stop at that location. Unknown to us, a CTV Television car had monitored our call and had set up in the area and was now behind us and filming the stop.

We positioned our cars behind and to the left and right flanks of the taxi cab. I was directly behind it and used my Public Address (PA) to tell the taxi driver to exit the car. He did so and was directed to run towards us at the rear. The suspect then stood up in the open front passenger door area of the car. My officers were on foot behind telephone poles as cover to the left and right of the cab. Our firearms were drawn, and everyone was aware of possible crossfire situations. The suspect just stood there and would not put his hands in the air or comply with any of my demands. I threw the microphone back into the car and approached the cab slowly with my firearm directed at the suspect. I pushed his body from behind against the side of the taxi and held my firearm to the back of his head. My officers approached, and the first two grabbed his arms and handcuffed him while a third reached around the suspect's body and removed a large handgun from the front of his beltline. Everyone had a task, and no one had to ask for something to be done. As quick as that, it was now over.

I now saw the camera crew and placed the handgun on display on the trunk of the car. I believe we should help the public see what we must deal with and use the press to our advantage. A closer examination showed that this highly intoxicated man had a very good imitation that day and the Detectives then seized 16 rifles at his home.

We were the top story on the six o'clock news that night. They had one very good video of my large silver .38 pushed to the back of his head. I don't know if one of my officers could have gotten away with that, but I thought a Sergeant doing it might be more acceptable under the situation. I never heard anything about the incident after that. The only thing was, when I went to court on my days off for the next few months, the other officers I knew would look at me and point their finger at their head and smile. Cop humour!

I asked and received the full rough video from CTV and used it for a detailed debriefing with my shift. We then saw that some officers could not shoot because downrange from them was a lady with a stroller. That was something some had not seen because they shortened their field of vision at the time on the suspect and didn't zoom out their range. It was a very positive experience, and they all performed in a professional and safe manner, as always.

LET THE MUSIC PLAY

One of my first challenges as a newly promoted Staff Sergeant and OIC (officer in charge) was the day I had two very loud Jamaican prisoners in the cells. They refused to quiet down and were screaming insults that could be heard all over the station. I went to my office and grabbed my portable radio and slid it inside the concrete echo chamber of the cell area. I treated them to one hour of very loud opera music and the second hour of country and western. I then revisited them, and we created a new understanding and mutual respect. They don't teach that at University.

SPANKY AND OUR GANG

Supervising the newer officers could be challenging. While I was at #13 Division for nine years as the OIC, I had many challenges. I recall one specifically. I had a lot of encounters with the platoon that reported off to me. There was an overlap when I relieved their OIC and my platoon took over on the road. This meant they reported off to me and I monitored their overtime situations.

There was one newer Officer that frequently tested my skills. Now Carlos was a younger Officer with only a short time out of the College. He was a very pleasant man, full of piss and vinegar, eager to please and loved his new job.

He was shorter than the rest, a little round in his appearance, and to me he resembled "Spanky" of the old Our Gang series, without the white dog that had the patch on its eye. He also had a great sense of humour, and frequently we tested each other's limits on that point.

Carlos was one that had a habit of jumping in at the end of his shift and taking that radio call for an overtime arrest. This happened quite often, and he knew I was aware of it. I felt he sometimes didn't give my early relief shift or the late shift of his officers a chance to take it instead.

One day he came into my front office to have a report signed before reporting off. He stood beside me as I read it to ensure I didn't have any required changes before he went home. I was reading a well-done occurrence report when I started to feel uncomfortable. He was standing opposite me with his hands on his hips waiting for me to finish. Then I felt a little "misty" and started blinking frequently. What was happening? Oh, damn! Spanky was unknowingly spraying me with pepper spray! I couldn't believe it. The red safety switch on his spray bottle must have been switched to "ON" and as he rested his hand on top of its leather pouch, he was pushing down on the top button.

I was in some real discomfort and equally annoyed that this Rookie was standing there spraying his Boss, ME! I jumped back and yelled at him to stop, and he then lifted both arms in the air. I wasted no time in washing my face many times in the washroom sink.

There he was when I came out. One very sombre-looking, embarrassed young Officer mentally questioning his future life on this earth.

Inside I knew it was an accident and I was sure I could get some mileage out of his blunder and felt sorry for him. I thought he must be thinking, "flight or fight." Now it was the joke of the entire staff at the front desk, and he was getting even shorter in front of our eyes. I just shook my head and laughed at him also. He wasn't laughing. This could only happen to Carlos.

A few months later, I started my day shift as he was just finishing his midnight shift. Like a good Officer, he was gassing up his police car at the station at the end of his shift. A good call came in at the last minute, and he wanted to go back out and get in the action and get maybe "an overtime arrest." The only problem was he forgot what he was doing. As he raced his car forward, he ripped the gas hose out of the pump and turned the gas pump 90 degrees to the right on its pedestal. Oh! Oh!

He is now in front of his favourite relieving Staff Sergeant. The one that he had pepper sprayed a few weeks earlier. He was holding his "Dear Sir" letter to our Unit Commander. Carlos was not wearing his happy face that morning. I watched for the Boss to come into work and grabbed him as soon as he entered his office. I didn't even give him time to take his coat off. I showed him the Memo and explained how Carlos is a fine young man but maybe sometimes a little too eager. His reply then was, "O.K. Shit happens! We will just fix it"

I made sure I caught Carlos before he left the building. I knew he would have gone home upset, not slept and worried for many days until he met the Boss during his next day shift to throw himself on the dagger.

The guy that he had attacked with pepper spray earlier now told him to relax, go home and sleep and not worry about this as nothing is going to happen. That smile had returned, and he left for home and bed. He was just doing his job and I was just doing mine. He was a good cop and I liked the kid.

JINGLE BELLS

Practical jokes were popular until someone almost got hurt. Have you ever seen one of those Christmas cards that opens and plays music? Have you ever wondered how they work? I did. I took one apart after feeling what a waste for it to play maybe twice and then get discarded into the garbage. There must be a better use of this unique invention. So, Hal tore open this card and saw a little chip that folds and its small internal battery. O.K., now what do we do with it?

I had some great Sergeants over the years on my platoon, and I felt we had a great working relationship. My management method was that the job gets done, but we try and have fun doing it.

Sgt. K. was an experienced Detective who had just returned to uniform duties and was enjoying his time on the road with the men and women of our platoon. One afternoon shift, he was in his office preparing for the upcoming parades to brief our officers and give them their assignments.

Sometimes Staff Sergeants have too much free time on their hands, and I was trying to figure what to do with this little musical computer chip I had in my hand. Then the light bulb went off and I knew what to do with it. Sgt. K paraded the Officers and prepared himself to go mobile as their Road Supervisor. I always sat at my desk, monitored the dispatcher's screen on my computer and kept an ear to the portable radio sitting beside it. He entered his patrol car, 13S1 (13 Division Supervisor car) and cleared with the dispatcher. He said, "Evening shift 13S1 is ten eight, one-man dispatcher." I could clearly hear in the background music playing, "jingle bells, jingle bells, jingle all the way. Oh, what fun it is to ride…" Approximately ten minutes later he must have had enough, and he said, "13S1 is off at the station!" In the background, everyone could hear, "jingle bells, jingle bells, jingle all the way. Oh, what fun it is to ride…" He came inside and could only find a staple remover and an old set of pliers as tools. He then went to the sally port (inside garage) to try and find the source of this annoying music. I followed him, and he told me of his situation. I compassionately said, "Really, oh my!"

He had no idea where inside his car this unwelcome brain-worm type music was coming from. I noted he was under the dashboard with his staple remover, and then he was checking out the roof headliner. I left the frustrated Supervisor to return to my pressing important duties. Maybe five minutes later, he was back on the radio, "13S1 will be heading to Central Garage" … "jingle bells, jingle bells, jingle all the way. Oh, what fun it is to ride…"

I had discovered that if you put down the driver's window, you can drop one of these music chips inside the rubber seal and it will fall to the bottom and stay there.

He returned to the station an hour later with the little chip in his hand. Sgt. K. had a garage mechanic take the door apart to find the source of his unwelcome Christmas concert. When he left it on my desk, I offered to help my former Detective with his investigation.

Now, I'm sitting there thinking, what a waste as it is still functioning. Again, maybe too much time on my hands. Around 10 p.m., the early midnight Sergeant arrived and was in the Sergeant's office preparing his parade sheets for his upcoming shift. I stuck my head inside his door and wished him a goodnight. He politely replied but kept looking upward as he could hear a noise coming from deep inside the drop tile ceiling, "jingle bells, jingle bells, jingle all the way. Oh, what fun it is to ride…" Knowing no one could ever get it out of there, I now wondered how long that little battery would last. I'm so bad!

THE WORLD SERIES

THE BLUE JAYS WERE IN THE WORLD SERIES. The first year our team was about to enter the World Series, we were all excited. Sgt. K on my platoon was a big-time Jays fan. He expressed to me his disappointment that he was about to leave on a scheduled Caribbean vacation with his wife in the middle of the upcoming World Series. I felt somewhat bad for him, but he was still heading to the sunny south and paradise.

I put out my feelers and made my contacts work and came up with a few sheets of paper and an envelope with the official Blue Jays logos. I contacted the Jays Organization and obtained the actual name of the lady in charge of the Guest Relations department. Sgt. K went off on his little vacation and I went to work.

Just over one week later, tanned and refreshed, Sgt. K returned to work. He immediately went into our Unit Commander's office waving a letter. I could hear him down the hall from my office. It appears his name had been submitted, and he and his wife had been selected by the Blue Jays Guest Relations office. They were to be their guests in box seats for the first home game of the World Series. He was advised to produce this letter at Gate

#5 and they would be escorted to their private box where they would be wined and dined.

He worked his way to my office and showed me the official-looking letter. He then went on to say it had arrived just after he departed for his vacation, so he had missed claiming his prize. He was very disappointed and further advised me that if he had received this letter prior to leaving, he would have certainly cancelled his vacation and gone to the big game. I think within ten minutes everyone at work had been told by him of his good and then bad luck story.

He retreated to his office, and it wasn't too difficult for my Operator and myself to listen to his phone call from standing just outside his door. He was speaking in a very loud voice and was now connected on the phone with the lady identified as the head of Guest Relations for the Blue Jays. He read the letter to her, and then he said "Yes" that he could fax it to her. My Operator quickly ran to the fax machine, removed a piece of paper and taped it to the keyboard of the machine. Sgt. K walked quickly to the fax machine, stopped dead in his tracks, and read the "Out of Order" notice attached to the fax keyboard. He looked puzzled as to his next step when suddenly the fax machine beeped, came to life and started spitting out a message. Dave, my quick-thinking Operator, came to the rescue again. Dave said, "Oh, it only receives and will not send!" He was a good accomplice! Sgt. K composed himself and told me he was heading to Skydome to meet this lady. He then drove off in a hurry.

Now this is when you think about how a practical joke can backfire. What if I was off on my timing and he had received his mail prior to his flight and cancelled it!

I can't let him go to Skydome now and sink himself further. I retreated to my office and had to pull the plug on this one. I sent him an MDT (Mobile Digital Terminal) message from my office to his car. It simply said, "Come back. It's a joke!"

He wasn't quick in returning to the station, and when he did, he didn't mention it at all. I was now feeling bad about the final chapter of it. I also thought he might need a big Ouchless bandage for the cuts the hook left on his lip. You got to be able to give it and take it. He later did get me back. Good for him.

PTSD

The stress on our Officers was of concern. Over the years as a Supervisor, I became aware of the stresses the job places on our Officers. Many times, immediate action was required to get them the care and attention they required. Times have changed, and the "tough guy" way of the old days are thankfully long gone. I was part of that experience, and we had to be strong always and never show a vulnerable side.

One of my officers attended a SIDS death in Regent Park. The tiny infant appeared so small on that crib bed. My Officer had met me in the hallway. I could tell he was affected by this call so I took him to the stairway for a private talk.

I sympathized with him but reinforced that fact that we have a job to do and must take care of our responsibilities. He returned inside and dealt with the parents, ambulance staff, and called the Investigators. I was pleased he completed his task, and I felt he had moved on.

I attended the hospital and noted that the two female Ambulance personnel had booked off with their dispatcher for some "quiet time." They had also been affected and needed a break for a few minutes.

I walked down the hall of that hospital (Sick Kids) and looked inside one of the treatment rooms. There was our little infant lying on a big stretcher all alone and looking so small in that room. There was no one else in the room. I didn't enter and immediately started to cry quietly. This big downtown Police Sergeant was crying alone in the hallway for a few minutes.

My job was now completed, and I returned to my duties. I thought we all were over our moment and moved on. I found out that my Officer had booked off sick for a few days, and someone said he was hitting the bottle. I had been away for a few weeks and returned from holidays to find out these details. He was now back to work, and I never brought it up because I didn't think he liked me and thought it best to leave it alone. To this day I felt, and still feel, I let him down and should have gotten him the resources he needed to cope with it.

Another time, I had assigned two of my uniform officers to an Old Clothes car for the midnight shift. They were shot at several times by a fleeing drug dealer during their detail. Months later, one of them, obviously suffering from PTSD, was involved in a very bad domestic with his girlfriend and faced criminal charges. I spoke for him at his Police Force Tribunal, and we were all educated to this new thing called PTSD.

As a Staff Sergeant, I have had to send out two of my Sergeants several times to deal with Officer's stress-related issues. Both situations involved sending the Supervisors to their homes to remove a loaded handgun from on top of the coffee table for one, and mental issues for the other. They had immediate professional help to receive assistance with the Officers' problems.

One of my other Officers had shown up for work and was weeping uncontrollably in my office. He had a shotgun pointed at him the day before and spent all night at home looking at his sleeping daughter. He was wondering what would happen to her if he had been shot. This was one of the strongest and bravest men I have ever worked with and probably the last I would have guessed to break down. My Sergeant spent the entire day with him in the office of a professional. He bounced back after receiving proper treatment. Two years later, I delivered his eulogy in front of over 200 Police Officers and his family when he died suddenly from a massive heart attack. That was hard on all of us as we loved him.

I also sought profession counseling once over a relationship problem that was getting the best of me. One day my Sergeant walked into my office and said, "Staff, are you O.K.?" I wasn't but thanked him for taking the time to show his concern. It meant a lot to me that he asked. That was a turning point for me. I learned that I couldn't keep it in and hide it. I needed someone to talk to. Thank goodness times have changed and immediate assistance is available, and there is no longer a stigma attached in asking for help.

DESK RIDING

As a Staff Sergeant, I would go out on routine uniform patrol. Being promoted is very satisfying, but riding a desk as the O.I.C. can sometimes suck. When one is used to being a "policeman," it's hard to miss out on the streets and what occurs there daily. I refused to go for further promotions such as to Inspector or higher. I chose to stay on the shifts and with my platoons for my last 12 years. Riding a desk is O.K., and I learned how to adapt to it over the years.

I could stay inside all winter and hibernate, but come summer and a good midnight or evening shift, I went mobile. I'd "advise" the Road Supervisor he could sit in for me at my desk as I wanted to see how the platoon was performing.

On one occasion, I could see a Sergeant's reaction that looked like "Why would you do that?" My response was, I must complete the yearly Performance Evaluation for each Officer after your comments, and I want to see for myself how well the shift is performing on the streets. I then added that would also give me the needed information to complete your (the Sergeant's) evaluation. In other words, if they do well, so do you, and if they aren't performing as I expect...well, you know. That seemed to work, and it was mostly bullshit as I wanted to just get out, burn up the roads again and play.

It showed my Officers that I did know how to do the job as well as a set-by-example method of performance. I would do it all from backup calls, alarms, domestics and, of course, all major occurrences requiring a Supervisor. I missed the car, and being out was still very rewarding for me.

During my nine years at #13 Division, I always made sure I got out of the Batcave many times each summer. I had a recruit on the platoon, Sang Park, and he looked shocked the first time he saw me out there, too. It was that "Do you need a driver? What are you doing out here?" kind of look. They sometimes forget how you paid your dues to get where you are.

Vince Elgar (now York Regional Police Service) was one of my senior Constables and a great guy. He called for me to attend a call as he expected some trouble to occur. There was a "pretend biker" also known as a "Prospect" from the local Outlaws motorcycle club that had caused some trouble at his house.

A computer check revealed we had a warrant for his arrest. Vinnie knew this would be a hard take-down. He took the lead, and four of us started to walk down the narrow walkway between two homes to the rear. I was in the second position and could then hear a loud voice around the corner yelling, "Get 'em! Go get 'em!" This short, stout pit bull came charging from the rear and around our corner. My Cousin Vinnie did one of the fastest gun draws I have ever seen, took a bead on this mutt's forehead, and started to yell back, "Call him off! Call him off!"

Well, I guess this pooch with the snarling teeth and growl understood English or the working end of a .40 calibre Glock. It stopped dead in its tracks and looked at Vinnie with a perplexed look. The owner could be heard calling his pooch back to the rear, and it quickly complied.

We turned the corner, and the fight was on with the biker. A few scrapes later for all of us from the bricks on the sides of the narrow walkway and we had him cuffed. My mind then reflected on the quick draw, and I said to myself that he must have been practising in front of the mirror at home. I'd have no problem if he had dropped a cap in that pooch. Sorry, dog lovers, but I saw his teeth.

Sang Park and Vinnie walked the handcuffed prisoner to the street and placed him in the rear of their scout car. We were talking to his family to calm them down and explain their options but could hear the "biker" screaming like a little girl that he wanted to talk to his mother. We were busy and ignored his request.

Then suddenly, we heard the loud crash!! Buddy had totally kicked out the side rear window of their police car. Glass was all over the inside of the car and on the street. I knew what needed to be done and immediately threw my scout cars keys at Sang and told him to drive my car to the station. I drew my Monadnock baton and threw myself into the back seat of the damaged scout car. I pushed myself down on the prisoner and used the handle of the baton to hold his neck in place. I told Vinnie to drive and I would "ride him in."

I could feel the glass on my knees, and this dude was resisting. The harder I pushed my body down with one arm from the roof liner, the less he could kick out. The thing I learned there about the baton handle was that with a little twist one way it would silence him and restrict some air flow. He would behave until I backed it off every 20 seconds or so.

My head was down, and I have no idea what route we were taking, only that Vinnie wasn't wasting any time. Finally, at the station, I assumed that the little behaviour modification had transformed him now into a model prisoner, and he was very compliant. I guess it was the closest thing I will experience to a bull ride. Neither one of us was going to be injured.

Sang Park met me at the station and gave this white shirt his car keys back. I'll always remember his look as he said, while smiling from ear to ear, "I couldn't believe it, my Staff Sergeant did that!" I told him, "Don't forget we are all Policemen. It needed to be done, and I was the closest."

Again, somewhat bullshit, I just wanted to play.

THE END OF AN ERA

It's was a very hard decision to decide to leave the best job in the world and enter another phase of my life. I was only 49 years old and had been doing the same job for the last 12 years as a Staff Sergeant, Platoon Commander and Officer in Charge of the station. The choices in your assignments gets very limited the higher up the ranks you go. I had always said that when the job wasn't fun anymore, I would leave.

The changes in Police Chiefs, Policies, Laws, Political Correctness, Accountability Restrictions and the general life inside the City and GTA (Greater Toronto Area) was making a negative impact on me. With 30 years under my belt, I was seeing the end of the tunnel. What could I achieve with another 2, 5 or even 10 years? There would be no substantial gain in my pension. I started to dislike life inside the big City and wanted a better lifestyle in a better place. I had two failed marriages, no children, migraine headaches, double vision after eye surgery from an on-duty car accident plus sore neck and back muscles. I had given them my best years and felt it was now "my time." I planned my exit one year in advance with a Financial Planner.

My last day was a hard one. I wore a suit and first attended our Police College to turn in my Glock. Leaving there with an empty holster was akin to being naked for the first time. Next, was my badge, gun belt and uniform at our Stores unit.

Now it was an empty badge wallet. They would return my badge in a month or so with a big word "RETIRED" stamped across the face of it.

It was the same with my ID card and a big red "RETIRED" stamped across it, never to be used again, other than for show. The next day I would not be a Policeman anymore and couldn't flash the "tin" ever again.

I was about to lose the inherent powers given to me as a sworn Police Officer. I was about to lose the positional power given to me as a Staff Sergeant.

I drove the unmarked police car downtown for one last tour that day. I sat just off Lakeshore Blvd. and looked at the Toronto skyline for some time. Flashbacks of younger days, exciting encounters, fun times, and good people. I drove past and stopped at several important locations. I visited Dibble Street where I had been shot at for the first time and survived on my tenth day on the job. I passed old #56 and #52 Divisions where I grew up quickly. While north on Yonge Street, I remembered, I looked up at the high-rise on Dundonald Street where a sniper fired down onto Yonge Street and I climbed out on a balcony. While working all three shifts downtown, there wasn't a section of street or laneway that I hadn't done something on during my time. It wasn't only Toronto Police I was leaving; it was also the City of Toronto.

I attended #53 Division wearing a suit as the Staff Sergeant, Platoon Commander, and Officer in Charge for the very last time. I joined my Sergeant on the evening parades and thanked my Officers for the opportunity to work with them and their dedication.

A few hours later, I said goodbye to my operators Mary and Ted and did what I called "the walk of shame" out the front door of the station and then walked two blocks east and had a beer at Hooters.

I drove east to my new country home. I had job offers, but they would have required me to stay in Toronto, and that wasn't in my cards.

There is good reason you will find retired Toronto Police Offices everywhere from Parry Sound, Penetanguishene, to Picton. Those hard-working men and women have earned their remaining years in a small town, quiet, clean and safe environment. Tired of sirens, shift work, gunshots and fights, they strive for the better life in a better place. I bought a lot and built a country home on four acres with a 10-mile (no, not metric) view of God's country. I have all the stars visible at night, and I can't hit my neighbours house with a rock. Here I am many years later and still have "confrontational" dreams most nights as my reminder of my best years in Toronto.

CONCLUSION

I am the person I am today due to the experiences and encounters during those formidable years with the Metropolitan Toronto Police Force, then changed to the Metropolitan Toronto Police Service, then changed to the Toronto Police Service. I am proud to say I was with "METRO POLICE". I could never have returned to my small hometown community and been a Police Officer there. It just wasn't my style. I would have missed all those adventures and opportunities gained from working in the big City.

I can't say enough about the best Police Officers in the country that I was truly blessed to be able to work beside. They love their profession, and all want to be of service to their community and make a difference. They want to make a difference, but the job has changed. The silent majority don't vocalize their disagreement with the loud minority that are handcuffing our law enforcers. We that have moved on only look back and appreciate the better times. We feel compassion for our comrades left behind for an unknown future in our loved profession.

We all started as young cops and I was lucky enough to enter the surveillance unit at a young age and see the world. The second half of my career was Supervising and trying to mold the newer Officers in the right direction.

Fortunately, I found surveillance or, more likely, it found me. In 1990 I applied for and was approved by the Chief to start my own surveillance consulting business. For the next 25 years, I owned Surveillance Consultants. This continued for 13 years while I was still on the job and another 12 years after retirement. I worked at teaching Police type surveillance (mobile and foot team surveillance) to over 1,000 Police, Corporate and Private Investigators. We specialized in teaching Retail Organized Crime Teams from across the U.S. and Canada how to work their trade-craft as we did in the Police following murderers, robbers, drug dealers and terrorists while doing police surveillance. Our clients were from companies like: Winners, Canada Post, The Bay, CVS, Simpsons, The Gap, Purolator, Loblaws, Securicor, G4S, Toronto Transit, along with investigators from Toronto Police, Kingston Police, CSIS, Military Intelligence DND, and many others.

Teaching only required me to work several weeks a year. My three-day seminars included 80 percent practical training burning up the roads all over the Province. It was very satisfying, and I was not only the first, but the only one out there doing this task. I enjoyed teaching.

In 1990, I wrote my surveillance training manual, The Art of Shadowing. For the next ten years, I was a Contributing Writer for Blue Line Magazine. My series of surveillance training articles were distributed across Canada, and further, by this National Law Enforcement publication. In 1999, and again ten years later in 2009, I hosted the first Surveillance Seminar ever held in Canada at the Blue Line Trade Show.

During my first year of retirement, I taught young law students as a Police Foundations instructor.

For over thirty years, I was a Policeman 24/7 both while on and off duty. I was given special powers, was legally bound to act properly and respond when needed to 24/7 and held accountable. It was an adjustment to a non-police life, but I have adapted quite well.

I must remind myself how fortunate my career choice was and the pleasure it gave me. I do know that in my final chapter I am now......JUST A CITIZEN.

LAST DAY: August 1st, 2003

Staff Sergeant, Platoon Commander, Officer in Charge 1992-2003

Appreciation

Thank you to my editor, proofreaders, and cover artist for your support:

Aeternum Designs (book cover); Bettye McKee (editor); Katherine McCarthy and Kathi Garcia

~ HAL

Enjoy this book? You can make a big difference.

Reviews are one of the most powerful tools when it comes to book ranking, exposure and future sales. I have a bunch of loyal readers, and honest reviews of my books help bring them to the attention of other readers.

If you've enjoyed this book, I would be very grateful if you'd take a few minutes to write a brief review on Amazon.

Thank you so much,

HAL

ABOUT THE AUTHOR

Hal Cunningham spent over 30 years with the Toronto Police Service. He has recounted many of his on-the-job encounters with other Police Officers and the criminals he was directly involved with. His many stories involve humour, suspense, drama and excitement making you feel you were right there with him.

His career spans the early years as a young uniformed Police Officer in downtown Toronto, as an undercover Intelligence Agent and then as a Sergeant and Staff Sergeant. You will experience gun calls, murder suspects, bank robbers, kidnappings, snipers, court cases and all aspects of what his daily life was.

The surveillance skills he used on the job also allowed him to teach Surveillance Techniques for over 25 years, and he is now retired from policing and teaching and lives in Ontario.

His favourite author is LA Detective Joseph Wambaugh, and his hobbies include boating and Texas Hold Em Poker.

He will share these Police experiences with you, so enjoy your own personal ride-along.

RJ Parker Publishing

Experience a thought-provoking and engrossing read with books from RJ Parker Publishing. Featuring the work of crime writer and publisher RJ Parker, as well as many other authors, our company features exciting True CRIME and CRIME Fiction books in eBook, Paperback, and Audiobook editions.

www.RJPARKERPUBLISHING.com
and
rjpp.ca/RJ-PARKER-BOOKS

Verified Facebook Fan Page
https://www.Facebook.com/RJParkerPublishing